FULL MOON ON K STREET:
POEMS ABOUT WASHINGTON, DC

KIM ROBERTS, EDITOR

PLAN B
PRESS

BELTWAY

TABLE OF CONTENTS

INTRODUCTION

The book you hold in your hands is a portrait of a great city's face, seen from many angles, wearing many expressions. It speaks of Washington, DC's bifurcated nature: both public (through its neoclassical monuments, museums, and Federal buildings) and private (through its neighbor-hoods). It speaks equally with delight and frustration.

All the poems were written by past or current residents of the city, who can best provide that intimate view, and all are contemporary—which, for the purposes of this book, I defined as having been written between 1950 and the present.

The excuse for this volume is a silver anniversary: as of January 2010, I have published the online journal *Beltway Poetry Quarterly* for ten years. But my interest in poems set firmly in an urban geography long predates that. I am fascinated with poems that celebrate the built environment, and Washington, DC in particular, which has been my home for nearly 25 years.

Many of the poems included have been drawn from the archives of *Beltway Poetry*. I wish to thank all the guest editors who have helped shape the journal over the decade, most of whom are included in these pages, and to thank in particular two: Andrea Carter Brown, who co-edited the special DC Places issue, and Teri Ellen Cross, who co-edited the "Evolving City" issue. Both Andrea and Teri helped me refine my ideas about how a city can be portrayed, and helped me select several poems that were first published in the journal and now appear here.

Decisions about what—and who—to include were influenced by a desire to portray the city at different time periods in its modern history and to cover the city's full geography. A few poems stray into the sur-rounding suburbs, but most stay firmly inside the diamond of the city's boundaries. I was also influenced by another consideration: a limit of one hundred poems. This book could easily have been twice that size—and I regret the large number of wonderful poems I had to exclude in order to maintain my page count.

Washington, DC is a fascinating subject. As capital of the United States, it sometimes seems like a "company town," where everyone either works for the government, or works for a contractor to the government. We tend to think that you're a local only if you have lived here through at least two administrations. And, depending upon the unpopularity of the current president, or the most recent Congressional sex scandal, when out of town and asked where we are from, we sometimes respond warily (with what my friend Dan Vera calls a defensive crouch), knowing that to outsiders we residents are often conflated with the worst offenses of dirty politics.

But DC has long had an adversarial relationship with the Federal agencies we host as well. We live in a Federal district that operates like a colony. Although we can vote for president, we have no vote in Congress, despite having a larger population than several states. The city's annual budget must be approved by Congress, and they often have different ideas than residents about how to best allocate our resources.

And certainly we are more than just government buildings and monuments. Our vibrant neighborhoods testify to a rich life lived far from the traditional seats of power. Our history encompasses the maelstrom of the Civil War era, when we hosted over forty military hospitals spread throughout the city, to the beginnings of the Harlem Renaissance and the jazz age clubs that sprouted along U Street, to the ferocious beginnings of the Black Arts and Feminist movements. We have been the site of famous riots in the 1960's and 1980's, have survived the era of being the murder capital of the US, and also limped through the pains of gentrification. We have generated great jazz and go-go music, and hosted terrific art exhibitions at the Smithsonian Institution and other galleries and museums.

I hope this anthology will help us, in its small way, claim our role in the country's cultural history. Unlike most major US cities, we do not have a reputation as an arts center. If we don't do a better job of documenting our arts community, we risk having our history stolen by others. That's how a movement that started in Washington would, in later years, become known as the Harlem Renaissance—a name that fails to recognize and celebrate our founding role.

I hope this book will give you a greater appreciation for the city's amazing scope and complexity. This anthology is a love letter to the place I am proud to call home.

Kim Roberts

FULL MOON ON K STREET:
POEMS ABOUT WASHINGTON, DC

MAY MILLER (1899-1995)

May Miller started her career as a Harlem-Renaissance-era playwright, and began publishing the first of nine collections of poems in 1959. Her books include *Into the Clearing, Dust of Uncertain Journey,* and *Halfway to the Sun.* She helped to establish the DC Commission on the Arts and Humanities, and ran an influential writer's salon out of her home on S Street NW.

The Washingtonian

Possessed of this city, we are born
Into kinship with its people.
Eyes that looked upon
Cool magnificence of space,
The calm of marble,
And green converging on green
In long distances,
Bear their wonder to refute
Meaningless dimensions,
The Old-World facades.

The city is ours irrevocably
As pain sprouts at the edge of joy,
As grief grows large with our years.
New seeds push hard to topsoil;
Logic is a grafted flower
From roots in a changeless bed.
Skeleton steel may shadow the path,
Broken stone snag the foot,
But we shall walk again
Side by side with others on the street,
Each certain of his way home.

STERLING A. BROWN (1901-1989)

Sterling Brown is the author of two books of poems, *Southern Road* and *The Last Ride of Wild Bill*, as well as a posthumous *Collected Poems.* He was a long-time professor at Howard University and DC's first Poet Laureate. Streetcars operated in DC for just under 100 years, from 1862 to 1962. The Rock Creek line went from Florida Avenue to Connecticut Avenue, traversing Rock Creek on a bridge at Calvert Street.

Glory, Glory

When Annie Mae Johnson condescends to take the air,
Give up all your business, make haste to get there,
Glory oh glory, get there, be there.

The last time I saw Annie on the avenue,
She held up traffic for an hour or two.
The green light refused, absolutely, to go off at all;
And the red light and the amber nearly popped the glass,
When Annie walked by, they came on so fast,
Then stayed on together twenty minutes after she went past;
And it took three days for to get them duly timed again.
Even so, they palpitated every now and then.

A driver of a coal truck turned his head around,
Watching her walk and knocked an old man down,
Old man's weak eyes had been dazzled by the gorgeous sight;
Po' man collapsed and he heaved a sigh,
Said, "Lord, I'm willin' at the last to die,
Cause my state is blessed, everything's all right,
Happy, Lord, happy, yes happy am I."

Saw a Rock Creek Bridge car jump off the track,
Do the shim-sham shimmy and come reeling back;
Saw a big steam roller knocked clean off its base,
When it got itself together, the little Austin had its place.

Ambulance came a-clanging, the fire truck banging,
Police patrol a-sailing, the sirens all wailing,
Parked any whichaway and turned their headlights high,
With their engines just a purring, till Annie Mae tipped on by.

Folks gathered from the manors, swarmed in from the alleys,
Deserted their pool-rooms, rushed out of their lodges,
Some took taxis to get them to the place on time;
Way the preachers left their congregations was a holy crime.
Twixt Uncle Ham's sonny boys and Aunt Hagar's daughters
Just like Daddy Moses through the Red Sea Waters,
Annie Johnson made a path, as she laid it on the frazzling line;
The dark waves parted, and then they closed in behind.

Aaanh, Lord, when Annie Mae lays it down,
If you want to take the census proper, better come around.

ROBERT SARGENT (1912–2006)

Robert Sargent is the author of twelve books of poems, including *Aspects of a Southern Story* and *Wonderous News*. He was actively involved in several DC literary organizations, including Washington Writers Publishing House, The Word Works, the Folger Poetry Advisory Committee, and the Capitol Hill Poetry Group. The neighborhood around Farragut Square has a large concentration of medical offices.

Eighteenth and K, Northwest

Over this parking lot, say fifty feet
Straight up, I used to couch for questions. No
Good answers, I recall. Old problem days.
And now, below,

I'm parked. And older. The building is gone, for sure.
And the doctor's dead. What's left is only in me.
If all those words had worked, things might have gone
Differently.

EUGENE J. MCCARTHY (1916–2005)

Eugene J. McCarthy is the author of two books of poems, *Cool Reflections* and *Selected Poems*, as well as numerous books of political commentary and memoirs. He served in the US House of Representatives (D-MN) from 1949 to 1959, and the Senate from 1959 to 1971, and ran for president five times. The main terminal at Washington Dulles International Airport in Virginia was designed in 1958 by Finnish architect Eero Saarinan with a suspended catenary roof requiring no columns.

Dulles Airport

Detached by Saarinen or God
from all coordinates,
it sits like a gull upon water
defying the subtle Archimedean rule.

The earth flows without displacement.
In this the only measured space of the world,
we come each a half two hundred yards
from shadow to form
from form to person, to meet
within the green range of each other's sight.

There at the center point, at midnight,
no arrivals, or departures scheduled
ticket sellers and stewardesses sleep,
planes and pilots are released.

Into this innocence of light,
not one eye of the myriad-eyed mankind
dares look. Let us dance, slowly turning.
We are seen by the immodest,
unlidded, unblinking, snaked-eyed electric beam.
The door opens out. Not driven
but drawn by darkness, we go
naked into the immeasurable night.

REED WHITTEMORE (1919 -)

Reed Whittemore is the author of eleven books of poems, including *The Mother's Breast and the Father's House* and *The Past, The Future, The Present*, and the memoir *Against the Grain*. He served twice as Poet Laureate Consultant to the Library of Congress. The Neo-Classical architecture of most of DC's major buildings invites comparison to Greek and Roman ruins. The Rayburn House Office Building at Independence Ave. and South Capitol Street SW was built in 1965, and named for Sam Rayburn (D-TX), who, at 17 years, is the longest-serving Speaker of the House of Representatives.

The Destruction of Washington

When Washington has been destroyed,
And the pollutants have been silting up for an age,
Then the old town will attract the world's Schliemanns.
What, they will say, a dig! as they uncover
The L'Enfant plan in the saxifrage.

So many plaques, so many figures in marble
With large shoulders and lawman lips

Will have to be pieced together and moved to the new
Smithsonian
That the mere logistics will delight vips.

For how can one pass by a muchness? There will be fund drives
With uplifting glosses,
Teams of researchers will mass with massive machinery
At the Rayburn ruin
To outscoop Athens and Knossos.

Dusty Scholars will stumble in, looking nearsightedly
At gray facades
Of pillar and portal,
And at curious acres of asphalt,
For clues to the mystery of that culture's gods.

Money of course they will miss,
Since money is spoke not at all on the plaques there,
Nor will they shovel up evidence
That the occupants of the chambers and cloakrooms
Were strangers in town, protecting their deities elsewhere,

But sanctums they surely will guess at,
Where the real and true pieties were once expressed.
If the Greeks had their Elusinians,
Surely this tribe on the Potomac had mysteries too?
—Having to do, perhaps, with the "Wild West"?

Like most of us sitting here now beside the Potomac,
They will find the Potomac primitives hard to assess.
Oh, may their ignorance be, than ours,
At least less!

ANN DARR (1920 - 2007)

Ann Darr was the author of ten books of poems, including *St. Ann's Gut,
Cleared for Landing*, and *The Twelve Pound Cigarette*. She taught creative
writing at American University and the Writer's Center. In WWII, she served
in the Women Airforce Service Pilots (WASPs), and in the 1940's worked for
NBC Radio. The Mormon Temple opened in 1974 in Kensington, MD; its
prominent white spires can be seen clearly from the Capital Beltway (I-495).

Temple on the Beltway Opens to the Media

Sustained by two bloody marys
and the look of the prophet about my host,
I took my introductory letter and drove,
slowly to be sure, to miss the ceremony
and arrived in time for all but the first
angelical choir rendition. Odd.

The angel Moroni stood aghast in the sky,
                        gilded and trumpeting.
How many accidents on the Beltway has he
                        embellished?
Saints and brothers and Solomon's oxen of the deep,
immersed in horns and polluted waters.
O God, the mercy flowing
from the mouths of the almighty
dressed in white and seeking heaven
through timid marble mounting
seven stories and no way to see
                out or through.
Royal orchids and fecundities
trailing ambiguities,
tithes and secret smiles.
                Do not arrest me,
                officers of the state,,
                silhouetted between spires,
                guns hanging out
                of your pockets.
I am aligned.
I lay down in the pastures of my God
                and was trampled by sheep.
I came to on the far side of enigma
                drenched with hot adulterous breath.
I longed for golden pinnacles,
                doubted them all.
18,000 missionaries are somewhere else.

Dear Editor: I am alive and well
                in the garden of iniquity.
You dreamers, scanning sin,
fingering the eternal,
something here is blasphemous.

BETTY PARRY (1927-1997)

Betty Parry is the author of a book of poems, *Shake the Parrot Cage*, and editor of the poetry anthology, *The Unicorn and the Garden*. She ran a reading series at the Textile Museum in the early 1970's, and at the Gunston Art Center in the 80's, as well as serving on Boards for the Literary Friends of the DC Library and Duke Ellington School for the Arts. Daisy Brown lived in a house at 1222 Kearney St. NE in the Brookland neighborhood. The house is marked with an historic plaque.

Daisy's Garden

For Daisy –Mrs. Sterling A. Brown

Down round her back door, the sun don't shine no more.

The day I walked the high stone steps
of your house on Kearney Street holding
the gloxinia I brought for your birthday,
you called it by name and it spread
profusely on your shelf, alert to love.
The deep green leaves of the bromeliad
flushed with red, glistened like fur
in the sun. On the eighth day after you died,
the edge of time dull and listless, I stared
at my nineteenth-century carriage clock,
its mute face oval and knowing. Though
I wound it yesterday, the striker is dumb,
hours go   silence is all that's left.

That and the smile that lit your face
and moved the corners of your mouth
as high as your clear light eyes.
Though hard of hearing, you never shouted.
Your voice echoes soft in the ear of memory.
Most of all, I remember the wild larch tree
on your side of the yard. How puzzled
you were that it grew as high as the bean-
stalk, leading to the clouds that harbored
the magic harp and the hen that lay golden
eggs. At your back door in Brookland, red
and yellow roses, splendid as an English
garden respond to angel breath and green.

O.B. HARDISON, JR. (1928-1990)

O.B. Hardison is the author of two books of poems, including *Pro Musica Antiqua*, and multiple scholarly and critical works. For 14 years, from 1969 to 1983, he was director of the Folger Shakespeare Library. The John F. Kennedy Center for the Performing Arts is located in the Foggy Bottom neighborhood, and is the nation's busiest performing arts facility. Designed by architect Edward Durrell Stone, it opened in 1971.

Pro Musica Antiqua
after a performance at the Kennedy Center, April 5, 1974

Listen to the music.
Listen to the sound of the krumhorn, the rebeck,
The vielle, the virginal, the viola da gamba,
The scraping and twanging celebration of order.
It is all in the best possible order.
It streams up through the air of your house
And it is like summer,
A kind of sunlight slanting through the dust
Of almost empty air.

Throw away the dictionary.
Live where you are.
If the sackbut palls,
Bang on a pianoforte.
Limber up the drums,
Unleash saxophones, let everything run wild.
Have voices, too, whole masses of voices,
Doing the Niebelungenlied by ear.

This is the way it should be. Your house should be music.
Welcome it, hold on to it, sweat, let it pour into you
Like an old god making demigods with mortals.
Hold on until your every motion is dance.
Having received, enlarge.
When you let go, you will snore in C major.

Percy E. Johnston, Jr. (1931-1993)

Percy Johnson was raised in DC and lived in the city until 1968. He was the organizer of the Howard Poets and founder of the African-American culture journal *Dasein*. Over ten of his plays were produced off-Broadway, including "Dessalines, a Jazz Tragedy," and, after leaving the city, he was artistic director of the Studio Tangerine Theatrical and Musical Center in New York. Pepper Adams was one of the most influential jazz baritone saxophonists. Club Bali operated out of a brick townhouse at 1901 14th St. NW in the historic U Street neighborhood from 1940 to 1954, hosting such acts as Louis Armstrong, Billie Holiday, and Charlie Ventura. The building is now the Arena Stage Costume Shop.

Blaupunkt

(choruses Pepper Adams never took)

Paradiddle, paradiddle flam-
Wham
A toot for Zoot
Six choruses for sweet Rose Cobb
Kadoom kadoom
Ahh Bahh Ahhhh Bahhh Ahhhh Dahh Booo
Bahht Dooo Toooo
Make your eyes go white on a
Saturday nite   like Leo Parker
at Club Bali for Paul Mann
'fore Korea—
Pound, Pound—unhuh-huh
Let Gerry Mulligan
make money
while you & Zoot
Make music.
A bahtt for Zoot
tsit, tsit, cymballlll
Boo dahh zummm

Grace Cavalieri is the author of 15 books of poems, including *Anna Nicole* and *Pinecrest Rest Haven*, and over 20 plays. Founder of The Bunny and the Crocodile Press and co-founder of Washington Writers Publishing House, she is perhaps best known for her nationally-syndicated public radio program, "The Poet and the Poem," now in its 33rd year of broadcasting. Key Bridge is on the National Register of Historic Places; it was constructed in 1923, making it the oldest surviving bridge spanning the Potomac River.

Mapping DC (1966-2007)

Walking out into the sun, we were coming closer
To the world of Washington DC. We were
Passengers, being carried along wearing a new identity,
Coming home to what would become home in 1966,
Passing through the locks,
Hauling what?
Only the rules of the road,
Witnessing the weather of what had burned away,
—That was half the time—
The other half was seeking new construction ahead.

What was there to see across the water
if our true nature was inside us?
If the inner city was within us.

It started with a sound, the sound of rats' feet scuttling
Across the sagging buildings
At the end of Key bridge
Where water touches shore with Washington DC.

Then all was silent as chrome, as the buildings rose.

1966. Looking back across the river, nothing was
Rising higher than the dirt,
No tall buildings, either side, in the beginning,
Just the sound of water. And traffic on the bridge.

Where did the earth go?
Into Sterling Brown's voice.

Where did the earth go?
Into the whine of the guitar of Bill Harris at the "Pigfoot" club.

From the highpoint of the Bridge, where did the earth go but
Into the sky, into myth and legend, into
Voices asking be let out of the jar,
All the voices—Black, White, Latin, Asian,
Coming to shore, across the Potomac.

2007. This is the end of the past with its sources and methods.
Voices are creating a new city,
Voices of breath, the breathing left on the map of ourselves,
Still to be heard,
As we sailed from the wilderness into our beginnings.

LINDA PASTAN (1932 -)

Linda Pastan is the author of 13 books of poems, most recently *Traveling Light.* She is a former Poet Laureate of Maryland and winner of a Ruth Lilly Poetry Prize. The Udvar-Hazy Museum, part of the Smithsonian National Air and Space Museum, opened in 2003 near Dulles Airport to exhibit larger flight artifacts from its collection. It was named for its largest donor, Steven F. Udvar-Hazy.

At the Udvar-Hazy Airplane Museum, Chantilly, Virginia

Here in this cavernous space
old airmen in leather jackets
as creased
as their faces, wander
from plane to plane

the way Odysseus might have,
back in Ithaca, moving
from ship to wrecked ship,
eyeing a statue of Circe,
naked behind glass;

or Icarus revisiting his wings—
reading the text above them and thinking:

so that's what the problem was,
the melting point of wax.

Here the Focke-Wulf, the Kawasaki Toryu,
the Enola Gay stand wing to wing
like killer bees, their stingers removed,
and harmless now
as the model planes of children.

Here real children line up
to experience weightlessness,
not the kind their grandfathers
are feeling—
the heaviness of time

momentarily suspended—
but the kind the astronauts know,
a feeling as curious as the romance
of war that lingers here
in the photographs of heroes:

Rickenbacker, his white
silk scarf blowing
behind him like a windsock,
wearing his leather helmet
as though it were a crown.

ROLAND FLINT (1934-2001)

Roland Flint was the author of nine books of poems, including *Easy* and
Stubborn. He served as Poet Laureate of Maryland and taught at Georgetown
University for over 30 years. "The Exorcist" was a 1973 horror film filmed, in
part, in the Georgetown neighborhood. The stone steps where Father Damien
Karras (played by Jason Miller) meets his death run between Prospect Street
and M Street NW.

Poem Beginning & Ending O)
For the cast & crew of "The Exorcist"

O
it was wonderful then

the movies (the makers) came to school,
o it was ivy xmas beverly all the way,
yes it was fibre glass and many special lights,
central casting at the Marriott Motel,
and yes sir starlets like Danish pastry frosted,
still glamorous, still cinemamorous
beneath the layers, and layers,
and when they closed the streets with a
"sizable cash donation,"
to the DC police club for delinquent boys,
and when, for scholarships in a
"large but undisclosed amount,"
they bought the campus—yard, lock,
and flying buttresses—
when they screwed the virgin blondes
for bit and two line speaking parts,
did another take on day,
and had the campus clergy
saying mass and eating Christ on cue O
(and when we saw at last how much we loved it—*we* loved it)
it was then we knew
they really know
what dreams are all about
O

GASTON NEAL (1934-1999)

Gaston Neal is the author of the chapbook *The Poetry of Gaston Neal: A Sampler*, and his poems have been included in anthologies such as *Black Fire, Black Power Revolt,* and *Voices of Struggle*. He co-founded the New School of African-American Thought and the Drum and Spear Bookstore in Washington, DC and worked as a drug counselor and a visiting artist in the DC Public Schools. He writes in tribute to Sterling Brown, DC's first Poet Laureate. One of Brown's most famous poems is "Strong Men," with its refrain, "The strong men keep a-comin' on/The strong men git stronger."

Sterling Brown

i've clung to telephone booths
in laughter
taken your hand in a park

and drank black whiskey
heard you cry and bemoan
the
young black bucks
shouting
a blackness
you knew as brown
saw you dance
the words
mesmerize the creation
talk a poem as ah human is
and do ah tale beyond the Remus
show
i have seen the green hospital walls
refusing, uncaring
about the nightmares
refusing, uncaring, changing sheets
serving meals, devouring strongmen
I have seen the green hospital walls
I have seen the strongman
caressing tenderness
I have seen the strongman
building the indestructible network
of an embracing love
I have seen the strongman bearing
white hot pain, spilling tears
on fire
I have seen the strongman
go to the telephone booth and laugh
                         and laugh
                         and laugh

January 15, 1989

Myra Sklarew (1934 -)

Myra Sklarew is a professor emeritus at American University, former president of the Yaddo Artist Community, and author of nine books of poems, including *Lithuania* and *The Witness Trees*. She writes about the Southwest neighborhood that was transformed by post-war large-scale urban renewal. Between 1950 and 1965, over 550 acres were razed, and modernist high-rise apartments replaced the old working-class row houses and small businesses.

4th Street, S.W., Washington, D.C.
circa 1913

1

How often I've tried to go back. Time's scrim
obstructs my view. The house: was it stone or brick,

wood or stucco? Was there a garden? Where
did the children sleep? Did they raise chickens,

grow vegetables? I did not know
my mother then—the way she and her sisters

swam in the nearby river, the waters of the Powhatan,
the Nacostian. Or off Haines Point.

2

Though I hold in my hand the document
of my grandfather's escape, his conscription

notice for twenty-five years' service in the Czar's
army, I cannot summon his face in my mind's eye.

3

A poet writes: "They've made me commander
of the dead on the Mount of Olives." I think:

they've made me commander of memory
until my own fails me. For here lie

two magical blocks on a D.C. street, the key
to my past. Before that, an ocean, a ship, a silence.

A few torn documents for conjecture. Taft was
president, then Wilson and a world war loomed.

The promise of Reconstruction broken,
school children divided by race.

4

Years later I bring my mother to 4th Street to see
the home of her childhood. But it's gone, raw

earth where a house once stood. Nearby,
the missing cantor's house, echo of his son

named Al Jolson and his brother Harry who sang
for coins on street corners to buy tickets

 to the National Theater, substituting jazz
for their father's prayers.

5

The doorway sealed behind my Lithuanian
grandmother. She set her sights west, first

to Bremen, then by steerage to America. She lied
about her age, her profession—not eighteen,

not a nurse, but a girl of fifteen, not yet anything.
By the time the Czar's army caught up with my grandfather,

he was already pulling a wagon in West Virginia,
a place where a farmer's son could almost feel at home.

They must have thought it strange to see
a man praying in their barns.

6

Like vectors on a map, life came to focus on a two-block
radius in Southwest D.C. in a small house swollen

with children. My mother told me once how
when her parents wanted to make love, they would lift

each child from the bed they shared and carry them
to another room. She remembered pretending

to be asleep. A brother, at fourteen, boarded
the Leviathan to wait tables, scrub floors and travel the world.

The eldest girl at fifteen joined the Naval Yeomanettes
and ended up in Paris. Two died young.

7

My mother told me how, at the age of thirteen,
she and all her sisters had to give up school

and go to work to help support the family,
how her eldest sister earned enough to buy a piano

and give all her sisters piano lessons. And how she
paid her way to Emerson Business School at night

and later to George Washington. Now I read
Shakespeare from her delicate worn books of those days.

8

I pore over the ledger books she kept for her father's store,
the ration books she saved from the Second World War,

and the photo of her father who has picked up his three-year old,
my mother, wearing long stockings and high button

shoes. He stands, sweatered, before a rack of brooms, a bin
of apples, a wooden box of Butter Krust Bread.

A.B. Spellman (1935-)

A.B. Spellman is the author of two books of poems, *The Beautiful Days* and
Things I Must Have Known, as well as the nonfiction book, *Four Lives in the
Bebop Business*, a classic in the field of jazz criticism. He worked for thirty
years for the National Endowment for the Arts until his retirement in 2005.
Blues Alley, located in the Georgetown neighborhood, was founded in 1965

and is the oldest running jazz supper club in the US, hosting such acts as Dizzy Gillespie, Sarah Vaughn, Charlie Byrd and Maynard Ferguson.

On Hearing Gonzalo Rubalcaba at Blues Alley

Prelude

among the things i must have known
but have now forgotten is the skill of waiting
the room looks beaten, used, abused
as a good jazz club should, voices
unattached, waft away from the discipline
of words to feed my agitation
there is vague music on the sound
system. it does not help me. my seat hardens
i squirm, i wait, i write. art will be here soon

First Tune

gonzalo is at the piano. a small sturdy man
all in black in the muted haze. i think
he is shy & will not speak all evening
except to name his bass & drum
his first chords fold back into themselves, spare
& new, adjuring the metronome. he knows
we know his flash & wants us to learn his silence
brushes on the snare lift a drive
into the tune while gonzalo hangs out at the back
of the beat where prez & billie lived, rolls around
in every chamber of the beat, at home

Second Tune

i knew he would throw it. all those years
of czerny wrapped in salsa inside bebop
swing him beyond convention. swift families of notes
sprint by in hard rhythms. right hand
firing threes left hand crushing twos & fours
I spot a candle
through my neighbor's gin. its glow falls down
with the blues. bud powell knows you, gonzalo

Third Tune

meditation on the run

Fourth Tune

that's a sunny day. some restless djinn inside the crowd
cannot abide soft & slow. it sounds like opportunity
to them. the conversationalists confuse quietude
with vacancy & rush to fill this new reflection
rubalcaba values so. they drop their mutter
into the deep blue rests he has made for us
a vitiation of a moment as close to sacred as i know
the way to & i must now listen through their voices
to his invocation. (but the song! How much for the song?)
thoughts so tender they can only be sung. rhyme in the nursery
said at the bottom of my father's voice in the last sweet
instant before sleep. (*that* song: how much
for it?) long slow unpunctuated lines drift on the barest breath
(how much (the whispers break thru) for the goddamn song?)

       ah gonzalo, this is where we live
       making lines, building space, hoping
       the natter will leave our silence alone

WILLIAM CLAIRE (1935 -)

William Claire is the founder of *Voyages*, one of the earliest literary journals
in DC, which published in the 1960's and 70's. He is author of *Literature and
Medicine: The Physician as Writer*, and owns an antiquarian bookstore in
Lewes, DE. St. Stephan's Church, located in the Mount Pleasant neighborhood,
has run "Loaves and Fishes" since 1968, one of the longest-running soup
kitchens on the East Coast.

The Jello Man on the Feast of the Circumcision
St. Stephan and the Incarnation Church

Mendicants shuffle by, sullen, accepting;
their eyes unwilling to focus on servers
whose food, like smelling salts, accentuate

the pain. At the end of a long New Year line,
I am the jello man, the jello man,
slopping generous portions of free church food
with my practiced, institutional scoop.
The necks that gulp like starving chickens
have slits in them, thin as switchblades
direct to a vein, yesterdays'
precise cuttings to the bone.

AHMOS ZU-BOLTON II (1935-2005)

Ahmos Zu-Bolton is the author of three book of poems, including *A Niggered Amen*. He founded Energy BlackSouth Press, edited the journal *Hoo-Doo*, co-edited *Black Box*, a journal on cassette tape, and co-edited (with E. Ethelbert Miller) the print anthology *Synergy D.C.* After working at Howard University in the early 1970's, he took teaching jobs at Xavier University, Delgado College, and Tulane University. Fourteenth Street is a major north-south road in DC, which developed rapidly after a streetcar line was installed in the early 1900's. Home to numerous car dealerships in the 1940's and 50's, the street was decimated by race riots in 1968, became a red-light district in the 80's, and a theater district in the 90's.

Taxicab Blues

I
this here white cab driver
looks into his rearview mirror
& sez to me he sez   "boy
ain't never been no
great
colored
poets."

i ask him what the hell
that has to do with
getting me to 14th
street
on time.

but he goes on like he
didn't hear me. "i mean i
knows for a fact that y'all ain't

never been to no college & ain't no
libraries in the ghetto."

and i think to myself:
man this cat is hip/smooth,
there's truth in his meter.
so i sez to him i say, hey man
how come a professor like you is
driving a cab?

boy, he sez, look here
i'm gonna educate your
black ass: beowulf was a
taxicab driver, bill shakespeare
drove part-time in a ford
and
anyhow
i like to travel.

II
a dc blues rap in a blackblack night.
stoned lerois walking these slum streets
pass me. 15 dollars worth of taxi rides
invested in the holes decorating their
old combat boots. storebought moonshine
passing from lip to lip & a long way from
home.
          somesay that they ain't nothing but
jivetime preachers talking to themselves,
somesay that they are the worst moves in
an allimportant chessgame, blackjack called
them the arc of a hank aaron homerun and
therefore a credit to their race, i asked
one of them and he said they were at the cross
road, bodies heading in this direction minds
torn between what they long for & being a social
worker for the army. eyes educated by the tales of restless
ancestors. he said they were the menace at the last
fork in the road. slavehearts throbbing hot blood,
dancemotion. over this bridge by freedom train,
on foot, by taxicab.

III, *afterchant*
sons of the pulsing darkness
sons of the living light
sisters of the struggle
daughters of the fight

mamas of the vision
fathers of the cry
singing

this time jerusalem
this time it's no lie.

JUDITH MCCOMBS (1939 -)

Judith McCombs is the author of five books of poems, including *Habit of Fire*, and two critical books on the work of Margaret Atwood. She coordinates the Kensington Row Bookshop poetry readings and teaches at the Writers Center in Bethesda, MD. Poplar Point is located at a bend of the Anacostia River near the 11th Street Bridge and across from the Washington Navy Yard.

Consider Poplar Point

These 110 acres of federal parkland along the Anacostia River
are D.C.'s last prime riverfront parcel— Washington Post, April 8, 2007.

Consider the river,
forelimb of dragon, framed from the sky;
drainage uncoiling; belly of tides
and storm sewers gurgling; gorge swollen with litter.

Consider the parkland,
a hundred-odd acres, lying trashed and disused--
a city's last chance for riverside views
rising like Oz, sleek towers on wasteland.

Consider the neighbors,
wary as snappers, weary of promises.
Consider the mayor, swelling with promises;
the see-saw of tax breaks, the floating of lures.

Consider the winds,
and the smallest of algae, and the osprey gliding;
the fish bellies, floaters, and tide surge rising;
and the dark man fishing all day with his kin.

Consider the access
to blossoms and pathways, to memories unhoused;
the sweep of the river, the seasons, the clouds.
Consider, citizen, whose parkland this is.

JOSÉ EMILIO PACHECO (1939 -)

Jose Emilio Pacheco has published 13 books of poems, as well as novels, short
story collections, and essays, and has taught Spanish language and literature
several semesters at the University of Maryland in College Park. He is widely
considered to be one of the most important living poets in Mexico. Sligo
Creek is a tributary of the Anacostia River that runs through Silver Spring,
Wheaton, Takoma Park, Chillum, and Hyattsville, MD.

Dos Poemas de Sligo Creek

1.   El Arroyo

El arroyo de aguas clarísimas parte los bosques
en dos mitades de luz solar que se vuelven visibles
en el silencio de las hojas.

Nada anuncia en el reposo trémolo que adentro
el sol ha gestionado la combustión
de los colores otoñales.   Así
estas generaciones de las hojas
se despiden del mundo.

No hay belleza
como la de una hoja a punto de secarse
y caer al suelo,
para que la tierra en donde sus restos
van a ser vida
sea fecundada por la nieve.

2. La Escarcha

Escarcha,
hielo que es casi tul o nieve de plata
en las ramas de filigrana: los árboles
que fueron y serán
(a diferencia de nosotros).

Es hora
de ponerse de pie y decir adiós,
de guardarse otro año
en el cuerpo que no da más.

Orden cruel u perfecto de este mundo:
la simetría
de los cristales
petrificados en el bosque muerto;
el hielo que ha de romperse,
la nieve que será nube,
el desierto
del *ya me voy* en silencio.

Two Poems from Sligo Creek

1. The Stream

The stream of crystal water cleaves the woods
into two halves of sunlight taking shape
in the silence of the leaves.

Nothing in the quivering stillness reveals that inside
the sun has ignited the blaze
of autumn color. Thus
generations of leaves
take leave of the world.

No beauty can match
the leaf as it withers
and falls to the earth,
so the soil, where its carcass
turns to life,
is made fertile by the snows.

2.   Frost

Frost,
ice that is nearly tulle or silver snow
on the filigree branches: the trees
that once were and shall be again
(unlike us).

It is time
to stand up and say good-bye,
to pack away another year
into a body that can bear no more.

Cruel and perfect order of the world:
the symmetry
of crystals
petrified in the dead woods;
ice that must break,
snow turning back into clouds,
the desert
of *I'm leaving now* in silence.

Translated by Cynthia Steele

MERRILL LEFFLER (1941 -)

Merrill Leffler is the publisher, with Neil Lehrman, of Dryad Press, and a
founding member of the Writer's Center. He is the author of three collections
of poems, including the forthcoming *Mark the Music*. The neighborhood of
"close houses" he writes of in this poem is Takoma Park.

Morning—Early Summer

It's not that I love this early morning
light that begins its glimmer between
these close houses anymore than I do
the high bright glare of noon or the sun's
last light that drowns in swales of orange over
the farthest edges of the city.

It is only that here, in the momentary
silence, before the glimmerings step fully
out from the borders of darkness—the rooms
filled with silence, palpable, your body in sleep upstairs,
the birds not yet claiming their territory—
I am breathing beneath the earth's dark skin,
tuned to all the invisible respiration
chugging like engines out in the backyard.
Full, complete,
at no odds with the darkness there or with the constant
feeding and being fed upon, a calm,
every need quiescent, still, ready
for whatever will come on and however
and the heat that will soon lay down its steamy paws
over each and every thing living and dead.

JOAN RETALLACK (1941 -)

Joan Retallack is the author of seven books of poems, including *How To Do Things with Words, Memnoir*, and *Mongrelisme*. She has also written and edited several nonfiction titles, including *The Poethical Wager*, a book on composer John Cage, and *Poetry and Pedagogy: The Challenge of the Contemporary,* which she co-edited with Juliana Spahr. She is currently the John D. and Catherine T. MacArthur Professor of Humanities at Bard College, but lived in DC for over 35 years. The unnamed movie theater in the poem below was the Janus, once located north of Dupont Circle on Connecticut Avenue NW, and the littered streets and lawns were in the 14th Street district of Shaw, prior to the neighborhood's gentrification.

Present Tensed

coming out of the movie theater the world the world is bright
too bright gnomic present tense tensile everything happening
at once the world is full of its own mute history the fatality
of reflection the fatality of nature and culture the fatality of the
German sciences of Kultur the fatality of i.e. mute history
remaining mute the fatality of of the preposition reaching
out to its object even as it e.g. it slips away

the preceding is much too or not sentimental enough to accom-
modate the experience of the child is fatally wounded i.e. the house
is a mess the streets are littered with trash the lawns are littered
with trash the grass is dying shrubs are pruned to look like gum drops
grass is mown to look like Astroturf replaces the grass up the stairs
of the stoop onto the porch into the house the noise is incessant the
grass is broken the broken glass is littered with people I have
a confession to make I have not answered my mail my telephone
my email my calling my God my country my conscience my desire to

i.e. what a pleasure to dissolve into the spot on the graph where the
logic of what people are supposed to know don't want to know don't
know enough to have any opinion on the outcome of another beer belly
bakeoff intersects with the logic of what people are not supposed to know
before or after the crime scene (has been) cleared washed down scoured
repaired reconstructed renovated restored rejuvenated retrofitted revenged
resettled unrecalled

also no not also there is memory as in trying to get to the fire the way to
the big light the photon points the way to itself

MICHAEL LALLY (1942 -)

Michael Lally is the author of 27 books of poems, including *It Takes One to
Know One* and *It's Not Nostalgia,* as well as plays and screenplays. In the early
1970's, Lally moved to DC to teach at Trinity College, and founded the Mass
Transit weekly reading series, and co-founded Some of Us Press. He lived for
some of that time in a house described in this poem, on Emery Place NW, just
off Wisconsin Avenue, near Fort Reno Park.

from DC

DC do ya wanna dance? You aren't perfect
but we know what you mean, remembering the glut
of furniture in the office—the problem is ours—
and even Kafka had tired feet! Around his mind!
And no one seems to tire of *that!* Howard Johnson
might only have been lonely, white like some concrete

or sand that nothing grows from except castles.
Like bones, or salt, "society's earth" once, or
refrigerator doors aging, waiting for hustlers, for what,
shit inside out, bouncing nerves about the dreams
he had had, his father the brick carrier attached
to the end of the cord waiting for the ice to get hard.
O, and clouds in that tender place behind her knees.
What were out real aspirations, that commission from
the child we used to be.

It is 5:27AM on a Spring like DC morning in March
and only now at 5:28 in what is everywhere still winter
do I understand Kerouac, or The Paris Review!
Alice fucking in our bed and Seventh Day Adventist Hospitals!
I want to let the world in on it at 5:29AM on Emery Place
Northwest, reading lovers stories. DC doesn't have to be
a museum in the pits! Spies! Ritual catalogue of dates!
Alternating friends, dressing rooms, cultures:
those eruptions of intra-human functions—grab a root
and growl, that's the seventies satisfaction,
perceptively recognizing two kinds of jealousy:
passion transformed into the uprising of the masses,
and the complex of human relations.
I jerked off to the Korean War
Josie hasn't been home in years
Everytime the Roosevelts touched it rained...
uncertain sexual stimulation. DC summertime clothes
make me feel like Christopher Columbus, all that land,
those high notes, we can dance, I can't sleep—12:48AM
70 degrees inside, outside a woman in the dark makes noises
like Ted Berrigan in Chicago, not the musical, without speed,
not DC where Ed Sullivan plays blues harp til 2AM with
the natural aluminum of a Santa Claus whose amazing cells
love to dance. Midnight December 24th, 1972, 487th poetry
manuscript for The National Endowment for the Arts awards,
check another self conscious crash, that's a, this poetry Christ
my throat like I swallowed dry ice I ought to, that must have
really been, sounded like something hollow
maybe hit into the side door, lighting a cigarette dropping it,
surprised and almost pleased, thinking, imagine this happening,
like starring in your own movie, not crushed, dead, just broken,
into the pain, my throat, most of these poems and the lives

if we can believe each other and after 487 it seems obvious
we can't just talk on the phone. That's what the moments do!
Pretense!
Wisconsin Avenue balloon man, Hecht's downtown store,
doin' the GOOD FOOT. It's the juxtaposition, the
"look I don't know about you" but I live alone with ten others
and folks dropping in on their way from Georgetown
to Bethesda, the place where things seize down, and
no almighty righteous fonts of magic fill the cars—
some dark invention to test the tension between
the tight fit of our need to star and that Washington weather,
like trying to unclog the toilet all day where A
tried to make her manifesto disappear because they printed it
wrong, or the car I let B borrow then paid to get repaired
each time, seven times, and she still asked for money for gas,
or the typewriter C used til it no longer turned
and the "f" stuck so that *life* always came out *lie*,
and I wanted to know if when they were through using my
books and records and clothes and car and radio and
borrowing my money and I was through making their dinner
and doing their wash and cleaning up after them and their friends
would they still hate me for my male arrogance.
With zest and bizarre little energy bursts
the train that speeds them out of the night, "eeeeet eeeeees soooo
bad…oooo soooo baaaad" because they've lost
the cosmic forces I give myself up most to,
that's what people call "performing"—
the best way to do some things is to do them the American way
cause they're American things, like beauty pageants,
sit-ins, phone taps, rocknroll, Hollywood and Texas,
where even the mice throw tantrums. This is the question:
did I? Slowly, like bringing the war into your heart
into the streets, making money not music,
wanting to go away but also wanting to stay,
and then one day to go away.

Barbara Goldberg is the author of four books of poems, including *The Royal Baker's Daughter* and *Marvelous Pursuits*. With the Israeli poet Moshe Dor she has co-edited and translated two anthologies of contemporary Israeli poetry. She is a senior speechwriter for the American Association of Retired Persons (AARP), and teaches at American University. The Dumbarton Bridge takes Q Street NW across Rock Creek Park, and is framed by four buffalo sculptures, two on either end, made by Alexander Phimister Proctor in 1915.

Once, the Buffalo

Why should Dumbarton's bridge be dignified
by two buffalo, their massive heads lowered
as if to charge, should one decide to cross over?

Frozen in that pose, their immobility turns them
almost mournful, at odds with this time, this
place where news travels by satellite instead

of smoke. Their ghosts still roam the plains
west of here, huge herds of them, lumbering
with a sober gait, stampeding only if startled

or attacked, raising an ocher cloud of dust.
Once felled by bow or drought or slaughter,
now acid rain dissolves their power. And once

their likeness grazed this land on nickels slipping
through our hands. Buffalo: they whose tongues
were prized for flavor and on our tongue still

circulate as slang for intimidate, bewilder—
even awe. These two are fated to be downsized
by this century's excess, mutating over our children's

children's lives, if not before, as headless, hoofless,
spineless shapes, impossible to recognize. What
will become of gravitas, the bridge, the other side?

GRAY JACOBIK (1944 -)

Gray Jacobik is the author of seven books of poems, including *The Double Task* and *Brave Disguises*. She lived in DC in the 1970's and 80's. M Street NW is the major east-west thoroughfare in the Georgetown neighborhood, running from Key Bridge to Rock Creek Park. The neighborhood is renowned for its many restaurants and shops, most housed in historic three-story brick buildings.

Forgetting David Weinstock

Afternoons of bed, of touch, of easy talk,
    slatted venetian light,

a bowl of floating roses on a desk.
    Copper evening radiance

on the buildings we walked past, late meals
    in outdoor cafés, the shared

carnival of city streets, all I swore I would
    remember, all

I engraved in my brain with the stylus
    of intention, is now,

for the most part, irretrievable.
    What did he say the moment

before I understood his betrayal?
    The loss is nothing to me now—

only his name sounds familiar. A heated
    argument, and later I broke

into his apartment and took back a painting
    he said I'd given him.

The Theory of Multiple Universes
    says everything is always

continuing in a world inaccessible to us,
    yet real. Each moment

of pleasure and of anguish, torrid sex
    and horrific suffering,

time and all possible variants, forever
        replayed. Does this thought

console or terrify me? An autumn afternoon.
        He hasn't yet said he loves me

but I hope he will, and I've brought a painting—
        he hangs it on the wall

opposite his bed. It's myself I want to give him.
        Slats of light through his blinds.

Blossoms of roses float in a bowl. On the tape deck
        Gould's deliberate intense piano.

He reaches for a pack of Camels, brushes
        my breast with his arm, stops

and kisses it, nibbles at my nipple. We smile.
        He'll finish his cigarette.

We'll make love again, then go out and find
        that Italian place on M Street,

dine in the back courtyard in the warm
        October air. I make this up

because it has vanished, because it must have
        been something like this.

Perhaps there were no blinds; that detail is too
        cinematic. Maybe it wasn't October,

but April. Would he have broken off
        the stems of roses and floated

the blossoms? Only a vague quick-flickering
        montage of sensations.

This is Washington years ago, I am
        in my twenties. He thought I'd given him

the still life: a pewter cup, three eggs, a lemon,
        caught in a sharp northern light.

MARY ANN LARKIN (1945 -)

Mary Ann Larkin is the author of five books of poems, including *gods & flesh*, and *The Coil of the Skin*. She has taught English at Howard University, Montgomery College, George Washington University, and the University of the District of Columbia, and is co-publisher of Pond Road Press. The Basilica of the National Shrine of the Immaculate Conception was built in the neo-Byzantine style between 1920 and 1959 in the Brookland neighborhood. It is the tallest building in DC, and the largest Catholic church in the US.

Labor Day at the Shrine of Our Lady

Breezes fan the Japanese maples
that guard the granite portals
of the Shrine of Our Lady
of the Immaculate Conception.
The Catholics bend into the wind:
the nun with her cane,
the pale hungry priests,
all the small forgotten people
whose eyes guard secrets
no one wants to know.

In the darkness of the Shrine
they kneel, to taste
the magic bread, the bitter wine.
On Labor Day morning
in the vaulted silence
of the church of Our Lady,
the spirits of the lame and lonely
rise up straight and shining.
The bells announce their passage.
Outside, tattered crows
drift in iridescent waves
across Our Lady's blue and golden dome.

TERENCE WINCH (1945 -)

Terence Winch is the author of four books of poems, including *Boy Drinkers* and *The Great Indoors*, and two collections of short prose. He also released three albums with the band he co-founded, Celtic Thunder. In the 1970's, he was part of the group that founded the Mass Transit reading series and journal. He writes here about three different neighborhoods: Adams Morgan, with its high concentration of Latino residents; Dupont Circle, which hosts an annual LGBT Pride Festival each June; and the neighborhood near the National Cathedral. The Kahlil Gibran Memorial, dedicated in 1990, is located across from the British Embassy on Massachusetts Avenue in a small park with a fountain, benches, and sculpture by Gordon Kray.

Three Addresses

1642 Argonne Place, NW
Alley of giant air conditioners, you roared
your ill wind our way day and night. We burned
you down, little house, but you rose right up again.
We played guitars by candlelight and sang songs to the cat.
We stole each other's cake and dope, dancing
all night, sleeping late, driving down Columbia
Road to the Omega for Mexican-style chicken,
which two lovers could live on for an entire day.
We threatened you
with a sledgehammer
if you wouldn't let us go.
Enough, you finally stammered,
be gone from Argonne!

1920 S St. NW: The Chateau Thierry
If you opened the door without thinking,
the entire neighborhood gushed into the apartment
like an open hydrant. We gathered around the black
and white t.v. like it was a tabernacle containing
the secrets we yearned to know. The first Gay Pride Day
made the building tremble so violently the roaches
scurried from the cracks and crevices looking
for safer quarters. Theordore, Edward, and Al
ran the only manual elevator still going in our
part of town. Casey, violent and crazy, dealt coke
out of his first floor apartment. Mara owned
a dozen petite dogs to be avoided at all costs.
Zoltan Farkas wrote The Baltimore Poems
and disappeared completely from the landscape.
I had a brass bed, my altar of love, and a cat

named Spooky. People yelled my name
up the side of the building, I threw them
a key out the window, and they rose
up to the fifth floor and through that open door
into my abode of bliss, which I still miss.

3701 Massachusetts Ave. NW: Cathedral Court
They told me I was moving to the geriatric district.
No Metro up there, they warned. But I was now
on top of the hill, across the street from
one of God's most prestigious addresses.
I would stare at the naked bodies carved above
the Cathedral entrance, like a page torn from
the *Playboy* version of Genesis, thinking
yes—this is the way religion should be.
A bus took me back to Dupont Circle
in three minutes. At night I'd walk home
up Mass Ave, past all the embassies,
loving to touch down momentarily
on Irish soil, salute the statue of Gibran,
great poet of wedding-vow love, hail Mary and Tom
and Cyn and Steve. Pick up the mail.
Waltz with Susan in the enormous living room,
then lie in bed at night, by the window,
hypnotized by the big cake of a church bathed
in rosy light, fireworks erupting somewhere
down the hill in DC's distant night.

DAVID MCALEAVEY (1946 -)

David McAleavey is the author of five books of poetry, including *Huge Haiku*.
He is a Professor of English at George Washington University. This poem is
set in the Smithsonian Institution National Zoological Park, founded in 1889
in the Woodley Park neighborhood.

She had a vision

she had a vision   not delicate but lovely   in its crazy way:
she'd come to D.C.   sneak past the guarded entrance   (maybe too easy)

leaping, scale the fence   cross the moat and meet tigers   her death in their mouths
she was a poet   of a kind, as imagined   poets seem to be,
and swam, I'm guessing   as all must in such waters   and is now quite dead

totally gruesome   and time's up: put her back down   gently as you can
the Post was bothered   *improve the security*   *if she'd been locked up*
(don't take me for true)   but lots of people felt that   (do me a favor:
find me a lawyer   if the Post takes exception: a really good one)
lots of people sue   for all I know this crazy   poet woman sued
sued left and sued right   broke and miserable and   no kind of friend left
maybe she caused it   caused each ounce of pain she felt   I vilify her

I'm not relenting: if she caused her own pain she   (sorry) deserved it
if she sued people   if she hid in the fringes   being so angry
I'm fine about her   she got just what she wanted   those huge teeth so strong
her little arms and waist   her neck cracking like a stick   her fresh gooey blood
the tender bowels   and inside her puny ribs   the stupefied heart

HILARY THAM (1946-2005)

Hilary Tham is the author of nine books of poems, including *Counting* and *Bad Names for Women*, and a memoir about her childhood in Malaysia, *Lane with No Name*. Mrs. Wei is an alter-ego Tham created, who appears in several of her books. Approximately three million visitors a year take tours of the US Capitol, which include visits to the galleries of the Senate and House of Representatives when either body is in session.

Mrs. Wei on Governments

In Washington, DC, Mrs. Wei takes a tour
of the Capitol and is impressed.
She tells her daughter:
"Malaysian Government is like the American
price system: take it or leave it.
It's easy enough to leave a dress hanging

on the rack, but a country is not something
you can get up and walk away from. Your Congress
resembles our marketplace: haggling and shouting

until everyone is a little satisfied.
Can we visit a shop where I can talk
the price down? I want to buy a victory.

I need a good fight."

MINNIE BRUCE PRATT (1946 -)

Minnie Bruce Pratt is the author of five books of poems, including *Crime Against Nature* and *The Dirt She Ate: New and Selected Poems*, and three books of essays. She is a former professor at the University of Maryland. The broken glass she magically transforms is in the Capitol Hill neighborhood, one of the oldest residential neighborhoods in the city.

Sharp Glass

Shattered glass in the street at Maryland and 10th:
smashed sand glittering on a beach of black asphalt.

You can think of it so: or as bits of broken kaleidoscope,
or as crystals spilled from the white throat of a geode.

You can use metaphor to move the glass as far as possible
from the raised hands that threw the bottle

for their own reasons of amusement, or despair, or the desire
to make a cymbal crash in the ears of midnight sleepers.

Or you can use words like your needle, the probe curious
in tough heels, your bare feet having walked in risky places.

You can work to the surface the irritant, pain, the glass
sliver to blink in the light, sharp as a question.

ED COX (1946-1992)

Ed Cox is the author of four books of poems including *Part Of*. A DC native, he taught poetry workshops in battered women's shelters and senior adult homes. In this poem, he captures DC's famous summer humidity.

Evening News

Summer,   5:30,   Northwest
Washington. Third day
of humid weather.
Stoops lined with young men
and women who drink wine
from brown paper bags,
                 sip on Cokes.
Windows open.
Drone of air-conditioners.
Screen doors shut.
Trucks back-fire.

A man, middle-aged,
stares from the second floor
of a yellow brick apartment building.
Behind him, slowly, someone drinks
from a glass of water.
He's thirsty.
That's the sound.

KARREN LALONDE ALENIER (1947 -)

Karren LaLonde Alenier is the author of five books of poems, including
Looking for Divine Transportation, and an opera libretto, *Gertrude Stein
Invents a Jump Early On*. A mural of Marilyn Monroe dominates the
intersection of Connecticut Avenue and Calvert Street NW in the Woodley
Park neighborhood. It was painted by John Bailey in 1980.

Against the Wall

For Norma Jean, Marilyn or S

At Calvert and Connecticut
she watches.
All I remember is her face
larger than a window
flung open in spring
that face floating
above brick, mortar,

and cement. Her bleached
hair expands the white
of her eyes, eyes that steal
light from the passerby.
Rumor says she shared
lipstick with my mother
as they strolled arm in arm
down a runway lined
with impatient men,
each holding out his will.

At Calvert and Connecticut
she beckons, what will
you do, she whispers
with petulant lips. Mom,
I shout from a café where
drinking wine with a friend
I glimpse the beauty
pageant, of pliant skin
and curving body receding
down the avenue.
With a playful skip,
she remains a child,
that child, Arthur Miller says,
whose spirit we cannot chase,
best to rest in place and let her
return with love.

At Calvert and Connecticut
I'll see her there,
up against that wall.

PATRICIA GRAY (1947 –)

Patricia Gray is the author of two books of poems, *Rupture*, and the limited
edition chapbook *Rich with Desire*. She directs the Poetry and Literature Center
at the Library of Congress, and curates the Poetry at Noon Series. The US
Capitol is the point from which the four quadrants of DC are divided. President
George Washington appointed Pierre L'Enfant to design the city in 1791; he
specified sites for major buildings and named diagonal thoroughfares for the
US States, including Pennsylvania Avenue, which runs from the Capitol to the
White House. The Million Man March took place on the National

Mall in October 1995, under the leadership of Louis Farrakhan of the Nation of Islam. Walt Whitman came to DC during the Civil War to be a volunteer nurse; he worked most often in Armory Square Hospital, now the site of the Smithsonian Air & Space Museum.

Washington Days

After reading Whitman's "Crossing Brooklyn Ferry"

This morning, standing on the sweet spot near the Capitol,
where tourists like to stand, I watched workmen heft bollard posts
into deep, cement pits. On this same spot, you too may stand,
deterred by the barriers today being placed. I imagine you, visitor
or friend, walking ahead of me in your future-clothes. You will not
know the Capitol we have known, nor the area generations before
us knew—when the grounds were open and citizens could drive up
to the steps, or even earlier, when horses were tied to wrought-iron
hitching posts that, later, were converted to park benches.

But if you have already visited, you may know me as the stranger
in your family album, the blurred figure passing through, as
you snapped a Washington memory—for I was born here: took
first steps holding my parents' hands on Pennsylvania Avenue,
the southeast side, away from the residence of power. If you asked
directions, I gave them. If requested, I held your camera, opened
the quick lens and captured you with the dome, its Statue of Freedom
on top—the same statue that was removed to the parking lot for cleaning—
a Romanesque figure with a helmet, and not the Native American
we had supposed. Just this morning, visitor, I heard, as you will hear,
birdsong and twitter, the scattering under feet of squirrels scampering
aloft at my approach, the caw-cry of crows in the distance.
And today, a cab driver may tell you old stories of neighborhoods
in days when doors were left open, cars unlocked, and about
Capitol Hill, on hottest evenings, when children in nightgowns
sometimes slept under low branches on the soft, Capitol grass.

Recently, too, we could walk on the front porch of that ediface
and look out over the Mall at the spokes of L'Enfant's city streets
leading away from its centerpiece hub toward traffic circles uptown.
Just a decade ago, I went upstairs in the Capitol on the day of the
Million Man March and looked out over the Mall from a small
window at the sea of faces full of passion, brotherhood, and

the deep urge to do good. This morning, as usual, dawn runners
hurry past, while others, dressed for work, speak brightly
into cell phones to no one nearby. Thriving and busy, the city
forms itself around Jersey barriers, metal check-points—though, still,
over there, you may see the Potomac's mild ripples where swimmers
once splashed, men fished, or others hunted its banks. And just as
the tidied-up Potomac sends its fresh breezes eastward toward the Hill,
the neglected Anacostia will also be cleaned. Have you sculled
the Potomac, or paddle-boated the Tidal Basin? Like many, I have
walked under cherry blossoms in April, which sprout from tree trunks
as easily as from branches, and touched the pink-tinged blossoms
damp after showers, glistening against rain-blackened bark.

Shushshsh, do I have your confidence? Come here. There is
still magic on this spot and—though the city can be cutthroat
in its clubs and drug dens and neighborhoods overrun and pulled
down—on any street near the Capitol, when the honks and shouts
die down and Congressmen leave for the weekend, you can hear
the soft scuff of your shoe soles on the sidewalk, and the city becomes
a simple hometown. Elders and youngsters come home. A mother
pauses to sit on a bench, lift her blouse and nurse the new infant—
its small hand, only a tenth-size of yours, while indoors, grandmothers
pad in slippers to pick up their newspapers. By now, a line has formed
at the coffee shop, where a Hispanic father continues to hold his own
against the day-to-day forces that, at times, would bring him down.

And, on any given weekend, while the media and cranes doze,
when you pass others on the cobblestone walk, look down
at the contours of tree roots buckling the brick path and remember
the poet who walked here and who tended wounded soldiers on the Mall.
Walk farther from the Hill, past the halfway house where small miracles
still occur each time a life that has died to the root sprouts again,
past lethal cravings. Then, you will know that freedom can return.
It is possible to step across rivers of fear and, with feet wet and soiled,
find the way, even as we construct barriers that hide from us
the knowledge that once this city was open and can be again.

Beth Joselow (1948 –)

Beth Joselow is a psychotherapist and author of eight books of poems, including *Begin at Once, Broad Daylight*, and *The Bottleneck*. Vendors often set up temporary stands in the Adams Morgan neighborhood, selling everything from jewelry to music CDs to clothing.

Stands (Adams Morgan)

They're a couple
<color> ruffled waist
bang ruffles, hem, hair ruffled in front

Maria de Buenos Aires
buy trade gold diamond
refillable

Two boys
guys with hair shorn
flat on top

Say it with style
he hangs around
her shoulder a big gold cross

Flores
donde
you don't mean it

To say the verdigris
doors on the church
where the guys lie about

"me too, dear, me too"

Tiny gold earrings
tiny ears
solemn trouper, a believer

Heshe with the long
hair, say, my pants
are long enough and my hat

And my bicycle.
Smile and stride,
speak rapidly

Don't speak—strike
silence in the kids
jewelry, general
merchandise, bus,
one with copper colored hair
blinking, silent

Police car
cuidado, Aquileo
de pelicula en hora

Microsoft tee shirt
leaning around old phone
barriers,warm
bold look goes
right for the eyes

Now dreaming in Spanish
and still here
a <cowboy> shirt

Paleo mio pink shirt,
pink skirt, Pepsi cinco
about the bright red car.

Some latitude attitude
my stand is this
take

Bandera slide across
the front seat, string tie,
por amor a mi pueblo,

orange nails, tienda santa rosa
Merenguemania
Tony Acosta y sus amigos

It's school, fat boy,
bueno,
today you stop traffic

Botas en special
Everything must go
chartreuse dress

Small boys with caps
puffed up
boosted blind becoming

trunk full of suitcases
astride those haircuts
Beverly Hills

bopboba bop rhythm
too sweet
for this

tuxedo bib on
albino boy,
gold again.

Respect, posted,
sheltered, wooing.
Strike that.

Chartreuse dress.

RICHARD MCCANN (1949 -)

Richard McCann is the author of four books of poems, including *Ghost Letters,* and a novel, *Mother of Sorrows.* He directs the graduate program in creative writing at American University, and serves on the Board of the PEN/Faulkner Foundation. This poem travels widely, following the path of a man in mourning; the part set in DC takes place on Columbia Road NW, in the Adams Morgan neighborhood.

Banners

After you died I thought if I kept walking, I could bear myself,

because walking was falling, one foot in front of the other—
I knew I'd be all right if I fell far enough.

There were things left to say! Dream-prayers,
unfurling like banners. *Dear world that is and world that was to be...*

But being dead didn't mean you could see through things—
not even through this paper, not even if I held it to light—

straight into the heart of my intentions! I had the sense of looking
for someone, though I was hardly even looking around; I was walking

the shoulder of a busy highway, or crossing a sand dune's crest,
or wading the bogs in the marshland, and suddenly I'd feel myself stepping

into an empty elevator that smelled of strong cologne—
who'd stepped off? At what floor?

That old mangled loneliness again, you might have said. Or was it an angel?
For weeks I kept spotting the mestizo busboy we'd liked, in a blue Trans Am

at the bottom of the hill, listening to Los Lobos, or crossing Columbia Road
against traffic, holding his young son aloft on his shoulders

like *Saint Christopher Bearing the Blessed Infant to the New World.*
Who was the one the dead send forth to hear what I would have to say?

It was as if I had died also. I could look back.
I could see the enormous faith I had sometimes felt

had been only a converging accumulation of little pieces:
through my window, I could see bittersweet puckering the hillside...

Grief seemed a form of patience I should learn. And then:
Were the dead really so dumbfounded?   So incurious?

Were they children for whom I'd have to unwrap each foiled sweet?
Were they even planning to learn to speak without me?

I'd mailed you a photo of myself taken on the beach at San Gregorio;
I'd wanted you to see me as I'd been, younger and more handsome...

But you never wrote even to inquire *Who's the man in that photo?*
It was as if you'd gone missing: *He came in a taxi, the first time I saw him.*

Did a taxi take him away?—All night I walked along the Embarcadero;
through memorial gardens, where black wreaths were festooned

with vivid red ribbons, like streamers on a girl's straw hat…
You who were living, you could have spoken to me, if you had wanted—

Everything seemed to be dispersing itself;
the body, like wind…

Or was I myself becoming—as they say—"a ghost"?
Through touch I'd sought what was communicable.

THULANI DAVIS (1949 -)

Thulani Davis is the author of two books of poems, *Playing the Changes* and *All the Renegade Ghosts Rise*, as well as two novels, a nonfiction book, *My Confederate Kinfolk*, and two libretti. Harold's Rogue & Jar was a tiny basement jazz club in DC run by Harold Kaufman in the 1970's.

Rogue & Jar: 4/27/77

> *the players: David Murray, Harriet Bluiett,*
> *Chas. "Bobo" Shaw, Fred Hopkins*
> *Poet: Ntozake Shange*

the "Iron Man" sat with zone eyes/a witnessing body
& a bad case of sky high low cold cerebral blues
the lady in orange came lit up with love and night blueness
David came with a gold horn/a copper suit
& Joann's Green Satin Dress
Fred came to do bizness/Bobo came disguised as the Black Knights
Drum & Bugle Corps
& Harriet Bluiett came from Lovejoy, Illinois 62059
the truth came down twice & i was caught in the middle
when it catches me i'm tasty & dangerous like one more for the road
it laid me out/it buried me after it worried me
it put ice to my temples & spewed out steam
it was rough/like playing with crackers in Cairo
like playin hard to get on Cottage Grove
it was rough like making love in wet grass
a heat that leaves a chill of remembrance

when the bottom dropped & the floor sank to the metro
i fell in David's bell/where melody is personal
the drum skin began to sweat burlesque
i heard it plead: please the ghosts/cast the flowers
the poem asked what it is to be a man
it was a rough blues/the truth came down twice
& squeezed me like a lemon/skinned me
& left a tingle there to taste
after such music there is only the quiet shimmer
the glow of eyes being handed back their sight.

LIAM RECTOR (1949-2007)

Liam Rector is the author of three books of poems, including *The Executive Director of the Fallen World.* He founded the graduate writing seminars at Bennington College, and administered literary programs at the Association of Writers and Writing Programs, the National Endowment for the Arts, the Academy of American Poets, and the Folger Shakespeare Library. Adams Morgan is a neighborhood of 19th and early 20th century rowhouses and apartment buildings that is one of the most densely populated and most racially and ethnically diverse parts of the city.

Twenty-four

Through the middle years
We took on the burdens
Of accomplishment mingled

Mightily with the sex-sauce
Of money. I didn't think
For an instant

About what to do
About getting a job
In the future

We've come to
Until I was exactly
24 years old. I remember

The moment,
On a balcony
In Adams Morgan

In Washington,
D.C., my hometown.
I sat with you,

Who held
A bachelor's degree in philosophy
And worked then

In a fish store, so great
Your love of fish. I loved books
So I staggered out of college

And worked in a bookstore.
We knew at 24 on that balcony
Unless we found other jobs

We'd be in
The badly paid nine-to-five store
Of retail (unless we actually owned

The store) for the rest of our lives, so
We actually let loose the thought
Of getting "real jobs." And in this

Instant of concession we knew something
(Youth?) (Fucking
Around?) was ending.

We knew something was passing
From our lives. We knew
The animals we'd always been

And wanted to be were passing
From our lives, that we
—Philosophy, fish, and books

In tow—had just thought
The thought we'd been avoiding
For 24. You went

Into computers (which paid
For a string of startling, staring
Saltwater fish-tanks at home)

And I, in years of unforgettable
Poverty and moving constantly,
Took too long finding work

Finally in the life of letters.
A good thing for us both actually,
To find the work, because

The children were soon with us.
And now that even middle age
Slips from us with utter rapacity,

We two old raptors sit on a terrace
In the Manhattan
To which I've come,

Our own children
Only a few
Years from 24 now.

They'll repeat that moment
On their own balconies, and youth
Will soon thereafter

Slip from them.
Jobs: youth-enders.
Work: the stuff of life.

TIM DLUGOS (1950-1990)

Tim Dlugos is the author of nine books, including the posthumous collection
Powerless: Selected Poems 1973-1990, edited by David Trinidad. Dlugos
was raised in Arlington, VA, worked for Ralph Nader's Public Citizen, and
was active in the Mass Transit poetry readings. In the late 1970's, he moved to
New York, and worked as an editor and writer until his death of AIDS-related

complications in 1990. The Wilson Line was a series of passenger steamships that once operated on the Potomac River between the Maine Avenue Pier in DC and such sites as Mount Vernon on the Virginia shore and the Marshall Hall Amusement Park in Maryland.

Swede

Michael Friedman's humorous pet name
for his penis is "The Swede"

I think of this because I'm reading
Michael's new collection of poetry portraits

lots of which are about girls he's known
and loved, especially blondes

and because I have to make
a reservation at the Hotel Suede

in Paris in the next few days
for my boyfriend Chris, a big

Midwestern Swede, and me
Chris would be annoyed I told you that

"I'm an American!" I can hear him say
"Why do people who grow up

in the East identify each other
by their forebears' place of origin?"

so let me correct myself: "a big
Midwestern Swedish-American"

whose forebears came from Norkoping, which sounds
like something people do in Sweden

something useful
and vaguely mysterious

the only real Swede I have ever
known was a girl who smoked cigars

and had a black producer boyfriend
her name was Jonna Bjorkefall

we worked together for a little while
in Washington a long time ago

Jonna's introductions to the mysteries
of America were the stuff of office legend

when she caught the flu and had to see
a doctor, she was asked how she would pay

"I'll stop at the post office on the way
and get a voucher," Jonna declared

another time, she misplaced a huge stack
of checks that public-minded citizens

had sent to help Ralph Nader's work
"Where are those checks?" screeched the boss

and Jonna replied, "Oh, I put them
somewhere," which I and my boyfriend

at the time, an English-American
named Randy Russell, thought was hilarious

though it strikes me just this minute
that both the stories are a lot

more humorous when you throw in
the Swedish accent

my favorite Jonna anecdote
is not a story, but a picture

Jonna and her boyfriend took the Wilson Line
down the Potomac one romantic night

I imagine them, she so blonde,
he so black, watching by the rail

as the city slips away and the darkening
woods of Maryland touch the shore

then Jonna walks alone to the prow,
lights a thin cigar, and contemplates her future

in silhouette against a backlit sky
like the greatest Swede of all,

Greta Garbo, going into exile
at the end of *Queen Christina*

E. ETHELBERT MILLER (1950 –)

Ethelbert Miller is the author of ten books of poems, two memoirs (most recently *The 5th Inning*), and editor of four anthologies. He is Board Chair of the Institute for Policy Studies and is often heard on National Public Radio. Elizabeth Keckley was a skilled seamstress who became the personal confidante of Mary Todd Lincoln. She later wrote an autobiography, *Behind the Scenes, Or Thirty Years a Slave and Four Years in the White House.*

Elizabeth Keckley: 30 Years a Slave and 4 Years in the White House

tall man lincoln looking out the windows
of this white house. i wonder what he's
thinking. the war not far from here. men
dying. death trying to get indoors. i rise
before his wife asks for anything. all the
dresses i make, everthing i touch is black.
sometimes i can't tell the difference between
war and slavery. i do my work and only forget
what i don't care to remember. lincoln is not
well, he looks old. his wife calls his name
every night. it's me who holds her hand after
he leaves. she talks to me like i'm a ghost
and not a colored woman.

TINA DARRAGH (1950 -)

Tina Darragh is the author of seven books of poems, including *Striking Resemblance* and a collaboration with Jane Sprague and Diane Ward, the *belladonna Elders Series #8*. One of the original members of the Language group of poets, she began writing poetry in the late 1960's as a student at Trinity University, where she studied with Michael Lally. She is a reference librarian at Georgetown University. Jean Toomer wrote *Cane*, one of the earliest published books of the Harlem Renaissance, while living in DC, and the stories and poems of the book's middle section document the African American working class neighborhood on Seventh Street NW in the Shaw neighborhood.

cliché as place — rainbows

The step by step process of looking
to rainbows
as a PLACE
for "pi in the Skye"
started awhile ago
when reading *Eye & Brain*—
the author tells the story
of Sir Issac Newton
pretending to see
orange and indigo
in the first color spectrum he made
so he could list seven colors—
a lucky number—
and this made me feel very fond of science
given that I myself stretch things a lot
to make them fit

so I started to wonder
about my other associations with "rainbow"—
for example, the Rainbow Tribe—
Josephine Baker being one of my idols
for adopting a baby of every color
but in reading her autobiography
I discovered some facts I hadn't known—
that she'd stretched things beyond her limits
originally deciding with her husband on four babies
she'd compulsively bring home more
eventually adding up to 12
the number of the tribes of Israel

and this numerical coincidence
calmed her down a bit
but by then all the money she made
was never enough
& she and her husband separated
& eventually she lost her place
& had to move her tribe to a tiny Paris apt.
from which she attempted a come-back

& I still greatly admire her
but this new information didn't fit
my image of her as the perfect
international mother

At this point I was reminded of Jean Toomer
having read his book *Cane*
I'd assigned him a role
as my "literary" patron saint
to go along with St. Martin de Porres
for whom I was named
both mulattoes
who felt they had all the colors
of the world's races in their blood

& *Cane*
written by Toomer going
from the country (Ga.)
to the city (D.C.)
as I had come from the country (Pa.)
to the city (D.C.)
reading his book in this city—
D.C.—where many scenes take place
people of mixed heritage
feeling at home
as if all their colors combine
to make the omnipresent white
of the government buildings—
the construction atop
the inner life surfacing here

But Toomer left the line
between Georgia and D.C.

& never wrote a book like *Cane* again
instead he turned to promulgating religion
through over-long works
in which he tries to tie
everything together

the only link with his past
being the repeated sound
of Margery/Marjorie
the name of both his wives
a form of "Margaret"
meaning "pearl"

& this brought me back
to one of my original questions
about sounds and geography
& I wondered about
sounds and the rainbow
&, looking it up in the *Rainbow Book*
I found that, yes, a physicist
Hermann von Helmholtz
had once "amused himself"
by comparing the colors of the rainbow
directly with the notes of the diatonic scale
visible light occupying
approximately one octave
in the long keyboard
of the electromagnetic spectrum
but, of course, the editor uses the word "approximately"
&, like the discussions of a lot of other relationships
to rainbows in the book, I think
he's stretching things a bit because
people have always used rainbows
for whatever they wanted them to be
the Hebrews saw rainbows as a symbol of God's favor
while the Greeks saw them has harbingers of war & turbulence
& the Zulus thought they were serpents who'd suck up
children and cattle

which turned me to the rainbow itself
one of many "atmospheric optical phenomena"
like the halo of 22°, the sundog, the corona, etc.,

all the result of water or ice falling through the sky
with random orientations
illuminated from behind
by strong white light
& what I hadn't understood before
is that a rainbow exists
more as a direction than a location
& that I must be standing at a certain angle —
the anti-solar point —
in order to see it
& that conditions exist for seeing some sort of rainbow
24 hours a day
for example—last week
we got back a roll of film
with pictures of P. & D. building blocks
& in one shot
there is a small arc of light
to the right of their building
& I'm not sure exactly
what to call it
or how it happened
but I do feel extremely lucky
to have been looking there
from the right angle
to that place
at that time

RICHARD PEABODY (1951 -)

Richard Peabody is the author of seven books of poems, including *Last of the Red Hot Magnetos*, two books of short fiction, a novella, and is editor of nineteen anthologies, including the "Mondo" series and three books of short fiction by Washington area women. He is editor of *Gargoyle Magazine*, and editor and publisher of Paycock Press. The Washington National Cathedral, also known as the Cathedral Church of Saint Peter and Saint Paul, is the second largest cathedral in the US, and was built between 1907 and 1990 in a neo-Gothic style. It occupies one of the highest points in the city.

I'm in Love with the Morton Salt Girl

I'm in love with the Morton Salt girl.
I want to pour salt in her hair and watch

her dance. I want to walk with her through the
salt rain and pretend that it is water. I want to
get lost in the Washington Cathedral and follow her
salt trail to freedom.

I want to discover her salt lick in the forests of Virginia.
I want to stand in line for hours to see her walk on in
the middle of a movie only to have the film break and watch salt
pour out and flood the aisles. I want to sit in an empty theater
up to my eyeballs in salt and dream of her.

When I go home she will be waiting for me in her white dress
and I will drink salt water and lose my bad dreams.
I will seek the blindness of salt, salt down my wounds,
hang like a side of ham over the curtain rod in the bathroom
and let her pour salt directly on my body.

When she is done I will lick her salty lips with my tongue
and walk her down the stairs into the rain, wishing that I
could grow gills and bathe in her vast salt seas.

BELLE WARING (1951 -)

Belle Waring is the author of two books of poems, *Refuge*, and *Dark Blonde*,
as well as commentaries aired on National Public Radio. Key Bridge, named
for Frances Scott Key, who wrote the lyrics to the national anthem, spans from
Georgetown in DC to the Rosslyn neighborhood of Arlington, VA. With its
graceful archways, it is one of the most handsome spans over the Potomac
River.

Storm Crossing Key Bridge

Seventy-five feet over the water, what stops you
still as the rivets in the bridge's arch is
thunderheads bellowing on the horizon,
under the bridge the swallows darting home, winds
riffing you with their pregnant
smell of rain coming, scent of a storm
just teasing a memory
too diffuse to nail down,

maybe something from childhood
before you could talk, happy
to walk on two legs, crown
in the air, sniffing the roiling
sky, and nobody hurts you.

Between two breaths   Now
you can forget
your best friend's dead.

Breathe, and the sky
dumps itself in the ash can.

Imagine nothing. Stop imagining.

ROBERT L. GIRON (1952 –)

Robert L. Giron is the author of five books of poems, including *Songs for the Spirit*, and editor of two poetry anthologies, *Poetic Voices Without Borders* (Volumes 1 and 2). He translates poetry from Spanish and French into English, is a professor of English at Montgomery College, and founder of Gival Press. Connecticut Avenue NW runs from the Maryland border all the way south to K Street and beyond to Lafayette Square. It passes the University of the District of Columbia in the Van Ness neighborhood, where it is served by a Metro stop on the Red Line.

Shadows Fall on Washington

This is where I chose to be—
the Washington Monument
reflected on the Potomac—
away from the Rio Grande
of El Paso, with its cool
dry desert.

I exit the apartment
on Connecticut
to catch the bus—
the golden oaks
and amber maples
are crisp with
morning dew.

The yellow
chrysanthemums
lining the streets
tell a story of
power and greed.

At Van Ness, I board
the Metro, gird myself
for the challenge.
Over the years
the stride has made
my onion skin
thicker for the task.

Now, twenty-six years later,
engrossed in my calling,
I bask in books and teach.
I've survived the
hot coals of K Street.

MICHELLE PARKERSON (1953-)

Michelle Parkerson is the author of a book of poetry and short fiction, *Waiting Rooms,* and a filmmaker who has documented the lives of Audre Lorde, Betty Carter, and Sweet Honey in the Rock. She runs the DC-based film production company, Eye of the Storm Productions. "The Throne of the Third Heaven" is in the folk art collection of the Smithsonian Institution Museum of American Art. Hampton worked for twenty years on his masterpiece in a DC garage, creating a series of altars fashioned from scraps of foil and trash, which was not discovered until his death in the early 1960's. Little is known of Hampton's life: he worked as a janitor for the Government Services Administration and never married.

Memo to James Hampton
*Builder of the Throne of the Third Heaven of the
Nation's Millennium General Assembly*

In our little privacies,
guarded and garaged,

there be tabernacles
secret and profane—

                  human.

They bear our offerings,
warm with slaughter.

DAVID GEWANTER (1954 –)

David Gewanter is the author of three books of poems, including *War Bird*, and co-editor of *Robert Lowell: Collected Poems*. He teaches English at Georgetown University. Following the cancellation of the White House symposium, "Poetry and the American Voice," by First Lady Laura Bush, Sam Hamill formed Poets Against War. In February 2003, the group delivered 3,000 poems of protest against the US War in Iraq to the White House after a rally and reading in Lafayette Square.

War Bird: A Journal
Poets' Anti-War Rally, 12 Feb. 2003

The massed and pillared wings of
the White House never fly—
            whitewashed yearly, they stand
impervious

        to metaphor,

to hawk and dove, and red armies
of ants. Only the halting squirrels
            investigate, creeping past the arrowhead
gates to scratch

        the Midas lawns

for treasure—On the street, commentators
wander like boys in a story too simple
            to explain. The political message,
a hat

        punched inside out:

once, the Nazis got word that Churchill
would visit Roosevelt "in Casa Blanca":
       U-Boats bobbed near the Potomac,
waiting for him…

     but Churchill,

as he said, was sailing to Morocco.
Reagan protesters splashed the Pentagon
       walls daily with cow blood—
soldiers waxed

     the plaster, and triremes

of rats licked the bloody grass;
the EPA sent health goons to stomp
       them, and the pacifists, away—
Then rats stormed

     the National Zoo:

urbane, patient inheritors of the earth,
they snapped prairie dogs like wishbones;
       vigilante zookeepers laced the ground
with poison,

     Carthage delenda est,

and killed the hippo. (Here, in the
New World Order, penguin and polar bear
       soak up ozone, and Nation shall
beat them both

     into ploughshares….)

Hawks and fat cats disdained
the White House squirrels, their proconsul
       Chevy Suburban nosed us aside:
we spoke

     against the war,

and for the cameras, spelled our names
on Chinese Radio—Elder poets shrewdly
        loitered at the lobbiest bar,
read first,

        then left us

to the falange of Secret Servicemen,
chatting like critics into their black
        lapels at every bungled line:
this was no

        singing school,

no falcon heard our crows and warbles...
Emily, our modest leader, rapped the gate:
        "Mrs. Bush wanted American poems—
I brought

        3,000,

all against the war. Can you take them?"
Gulping, the pimply guard asked his shirt
        for help; older hands hustled up,
"The Great Oz

        cannot see you..." etc.

Will four and twenty blackbirds fill
a cowboy hat? Bunkered belowdecks,
        the President goes for the burn,
racing the

        cut tongue

of his treadmill to a dead heat.
Even Nixon met the enemy once,
        strode with his staff into a red sea
of hippies—

        they didn't part,

and he burbled about baseball…
from his desk, he liked to watch
          the sightseers through a gap
in the hedges;

          peaceniks

learned this and blocked his view,
stood there day and night for years:
          Nixon, nightmare reality shanking
through his eyes,

          knelt with Kissinger:

Henry, he moaned, *what do they want?*….
Days from now, how many days,
          the Valentine "Woo at the Zoo" begins.
A hand-raised

          falcon bows,

and shares meat with its master.…
He bows in turn, and eats;
          both softly whisper *ee-chu,*
ee-chu,

          a duet

heard only on abstract and crumbling
cliffs—if a man were to stand or
          sing there, he'd fall. The master
straps on a

          a falcon feathered

courtesan's hat and turns away—
Flapping wildly, the falcon claws
          the head-shape, squawking,
gyrating to

          hold on,

imperial lunge and lunge,
biting at the skull it fed, as
semen slowly drips into a
rubber dam.

Sunil Freeman (1955 -)

Sunil Freeman is the author of two books of poems, *That Would Explain the Violinist*, and *Surreal Freedom Blues*. He is Assistant Director of The Writer's Center in Bethesda, MD and DC Branch Bureau web editor for the Party for Socialism and Liberation. The expansive open lawns of the National Mall are surrounded by museums and monuments, anchored on the east by the US Capitol and the west by the Lincoln Memorial. Administered by the National Park Service, the Mall is a civic stage, hosting protests, festivals (such as the Smithsonian Folklife Festival and the National Book Festival), presidential inaugurations, and serving approximately 25 million annual visitors.

The Cinematographer's Dream
The Mall, Washington, D.C.
February, 1992

Sunshine does its old Vermeer embrace,
washing over the flats to the west.
It highlights a long touchdown pass,
then rolls back to catch the whole field
and bathe both teams till they might be
the first Olympians. The light rides
on shafts of its own finding, little ripples
over the grass, a beam that slants
and cuts like a halfback. I watch
this wanton grace, and then the tourists,

who see with eyes of pilgrimage
as they climb the slow incline.
Their chatter highlights the hush
that enfolds us inside the ring road
at the summit, the monument's base.
We all look to clouds that circle
the landscape. There should be chords
humming deep in those cumulus hearts;
they ride a wind that shatters

around us into bright metallic clicks
inside the crackling of flags.

To the east, a thin Black man plays
a pop tune lifted from the Andes.
His flute is a marriage of gray and silver
that's echoed by his tin can,
and by the quarter that flares,
briefly, then softens, shyly,
as it leaves a stranger's hand.

MILES DAVID MOORE (1955 –)

Miles David Moore is a Washington reporter for Crain Communications, the founder of the Iota Poetry Series in Arlington, and the author of three books of poems, most recently *Rollercoaster.* K Street NW is a major thoroughfare in downtown DC famous as the home to law firms and government lobbyists.

Full Moon on K Street

The moon has your face tonight,
hiding behind black-violet veils
of clouds, coy, intimating nothing.

Like an orange outside the grasp
of a starving child, you stab my heart.
All longing is the same.

No natural light penetrates
this street; the lampposts rule.
The high-rises have mothered

them from their concrete wombs,
bidding us rejoice in coldness,
disdaining the celestial tease.

The moon has phases. Though I pray
not, you might be one. The clouds
pull tight, tight around your mouth.

DONNA DENIZÉ (1955 –)

Donna Denizé is the author of two books of poems, most recently *Broken Like Job*. She is Chair of the English Department at St. Albans School for Boys, on the campus of the National Cathedral. Pulpit Rock is an outcropping with a dramatic view overlooking Rock Creek on the Teddy Roosevelt Trail in Rock Creek Park, a National Park Service site that runs from north to south through the middle of the city.

Pulpit Rock (in Rock Creek Park)

Here I recall Sampson, blind, led to a temple's central pillars that he might lean
against them and pull the edifice down, or Moses who led the way, as a pillar of fire

gave them light, that they might travel by night. So, too this trail leads and converges
at a peak, no ministers or sermons, just one slender natural formation

named *Pillar,* standing alone, and I believe in this forest of ridge tops, slopes,
sandy loam and rocky soil, this plateau of green, of tall forest trees—chestnut oak

and black gum—canopy of sassafras, serviceberry, tall shrubs and greenbrier vines.
    Amidst
shrubs, heaths of blueberry and huckleberry, mountain laurel and azalea, I believe

in the climb, the two mile trail to mountain *Pillar— Pulpit Rock—* overlooking the
    Creek,
this place of roots and rocks, remnants of cobblestone roads and passing sounds of deer

and joggers. I believe in this ravine, in gently sloping hills by one limpid stream along
    the fall
line, believe in this rolling plain's seaward slope that disappears till we are nothing,
    nothing

but ear longing to hear, hear what Moses heard captivating on crippling climb
and rapturous rise to heart's summit when He, all ears, stood listening

to Voice that carried Him away, reducing all other mountains to dust. So it is here
where I recall the limitless ocean of billowing seas, one Common Script, favoring fires,

and peaks of understanding—knowing who we are
and may become—and so I believe in ridges that rise

above the Plain, provinces closely aligned, and all rigorous trails
along streams and upland mountains.

BRANDON D. JOHNSON (1955-)

Brandon D. Johnson is the author of three books of poems, including *Love's Skin*, and is included in such anthologies as *The Black Rooster Social Inn: This is the Place, Cabin Fever*, and *Gathering Ground*. P Street NW runs through the Shaw neighborhood. Ben's Chili Bowl is a city landmark, serving patrons its famous chili smokes on U Street since 1958.

Displaced Person

you are not secluded
behind those oversized shades
you have nothing to hide
under your processed mop
reddened by its time in the sun
your thin sideburns trailing
the edge of your jawbone aren't
a masterwork to conceal
but the fact that you're
not piloting a pimpmobile
down "P" in '68, that your
stacked heels aren't cruising
you to Ben's Chili Bowl and the best pimpsteak
in the city at two in the morning
that you're riding this subway with me
thirty years after what appears to be
your time
i can only wonder which train
of life, or thought, left you
behind.

MICHAEL GUSHUE (1955 -)

Michael Gushue is the author of a book of poems, *Gathering Down Women*, publisher of Beothuk Books, and co-publisher of Vrzhu Press. He co-curates the Brookland Poetry Reading Series. The intersection of North Capitol and New York Avenues is an area of urban blight; the only businesses that seem to be able to prosper there are liquor stores.

Big Ben's Liquors
N. Capitol and New York Avenues

Can you spare a quarter for a lucid moment?
There was the time my cash flow went dingo on me,
the time Mom gave me that look, that hard rain fell.
Have you ever been gut shot by a wrong turn?

As a safe bet, try to stall between stations,
hope to forget how bright the spot's glare is,
rather than face having to endure stopping
on a dime. But "hope to forget" is too glistening

a phrase: nobody hears it. It would be better
to wrap it like one of the homeless in felt
blankets, send it piebald to the streets and grates
and let it beg on its poor twisting feet for nickels.

It's a sure bet no one gives a plug nickel
for your thoughts, and, even more, no one
ever says "a penny for your feelings"--that's
economics for you. That's when I hold up a sign

saying: Will Work for Lucidity. Some people
find it sad, but I have to hurry to be sad or
I'll be late for being lucid and catch hell,
which hurts like hell, wakes me up, thinking:

how do we endure being full of these felt
moments: flares of brief joy, heart cut by birdsong,
a funnel of lamplight filled with snow, or the fourth
thing has slipped my mind: a sudden radio station

in the middle of a trip from K Street to Michigan,
lottery stubs carpeting the liquor store pavement
and pulling taut, speaking in their own voice: this
is the most important bet that you will ever lose.

JONETTA ROSE BARRAS (1956 -)

Jonetta Rose Barras is the author of a poetry collection, *The Corner Is No Place for Hiding*, and three nonfiction books, including *Bridges: Reuniting Daughters and Daddies*. She is an award-winning journalist and political analyst who writes a twice-weekly column for the *Washington Examiner* and is a frequent contributor to the *Washington Post*. In this poem, she captures the lack of safety residents felt in the 1980's and 90's, when DC was known as the "murder capital."

There's Been a Killing in the Neighborhood

a wreath goes up
a slant-eyes boy runs
trying to catch the gunshots
stuff them back
into the iron that released them
should i panic
put up more bars
on the barred windows
buy a 9 mm
light a candle to
shango or some other diety
there must be something
i can do.

there's been a killing in the neighborhood.

did someone come
from the outside or
was it someone who
greeted her each morning
the bullet hiding behind
a smile?

two in the afternoon
the sound came

from her mouth
the language strange
and staggering
the hole opened up
in her small body
i was not there to see
the blood running
from the counter where
my paper and bread once lay
to the curb where i catch
the H2 bus moving
somewhere in the city
someone is counting change
maybe flashing bills
while i sit
at this barred window wondering
who will be next.

ESSEX HEMPHILL (1957-1995)

Essex Hemphill is the author of two books of poems, *Ceremonies* and
Conditions, and the editor of the anthology *Brother to Brother: New Writings
by Black Gay Men*. An activist who worked for gay rights, he also appeared
in several films. The neighborhoods of the Southeast quadrant of DC,
particularly those east of the Anacostia River, have often felt separate from
the rest of the city, with fewer basic amenities (such as shopping, dining,
health care, transportation, and cultural facilities).

Family Jewels

for Washington D.C.

I live in a town
where pretense and bone structure
prevail as credentials
of status and beauty.
A town bewitched
by mirrors, horoscopes
and corruption.

I intrude on this nightmare.
Arm outstretched from curbside.
I'm not pointing to Zimbabwe.

I want a cab
to take me to Southeast
so I can visit my mother.
I'm not ashamed to cross
the bridge that takes me there.

No matter where I live
or what I wear
the cabs speed by.
Or they suddenly brake
a few feet away
spewing fumes in my face
to serve a fair skinned fare.
I live in a town
where everyone is afraid
of the dark.
I stand my ground unarmed
facing a mounting disrespect,
a diminishing patience,
a need for defense.

In passing headlights
I appear to be a criminal.
I'm a weird looking muthafucka.
Shaggy green hair sprouts all over me.
My shoulders hunch and bulge. I growl
as blood drips from my glinting fangs.

My mother's flowers are wilting
while I wait.
Our dinner
is cold by now.

I live in a town
where pretense and structure
are devices of cruelty.
A town bewitched
by mirrors, horoscopes
and blood.

JOSE PADUA (1957 -)

Jose Padua grew up in DC, and has performed his poetry widely, in such places as the Lollapalooza Festival, CBGBs, and the Washington Project for the Arts. His features and reviews have appeared in *NYPress*, *Washington City Paper, Brooklyn Rail,* and *The New York Times*. Chief Ike's Mambo Room is a bar that opened in 1991 on Columbia Road NW in the Adams Morgan neighborhood.

1996

In 1995 I ate one hundred steaks, drank 1,298 beers,
and saw two movies— "Pulp Fiction" and "Speed."

In 1995 I walked 1,223 miles in the sun, rain, and
sometimes snow, casting evil looks at 99% of the

people who looked my way and smiling behind
the backs of the remaining 1%. I bought 10,940

cigarettes, gave 146 of them to friends, 16 to
strangers, and lost 2 on the wet bathroom floor of

Chief Ike's Mambo Room. The days went quickly.
Some of them I remember, some of them I don't.

In 1996 you took me away from my old numbers.
When we walk I don't count the miles. And though

I still hate much of the world I am no longer
bitter about it because you are here in mine.

JOSEPH ROSS (1958 -)

Joseph Ross teaches in the College Writing Program at American University, and is co-editor of the anthology *Cut Loose the Body*. Beginning in the 1990's, downtown Silver Spring, MD began a redevelopment program to improve the streetscape and encourage new development.

The Universal Artificial Limb Company

The Universal Artificial Limb Company
crouches at the end
of a row of storefronts.
It waits on Wayne Avenue
at the end of a strip mall
whose other stores
are long since closed,
their windows covered
with brown paper and plywood,
like women draped in mourning veils.

Its marketing plan looks like modesty
which these days
does not really sell.

Its name, painted in clean
gold and black letters,
arcs across the front window,
announcing the ancient art
of remembering what has been
dismembered.

Meanwhile, Whole Foods and Starbucks
hover across the street
waiting, plotting, maybe even grinning,
rubbing their manicured hands together
under tasteful signs,
beside stacks of polished fruit
picked by people
who knew what it meant
to bend.

Next door, luxury condos
rise slowly, floor by floor,
a high-rise with the perfect posture
to look down at a store
not even sophisticated enough
to call its product prosthetics.

The Universal Artificial Limb Company
must be careful.
It tries to stay wary,
it tries to deflect the muscled arms
that would shove it aside
in favor of a market more whole,
more hip,
whose reach extends well beyond
the noble hope of healing
both members and memory.

GREGG SHAPIRO (1959 -)

Gregg Shapiro is an entertainment journalist and the author of a book of poems, *Protection*. He lived in DC in the 1980's. Chinatown is a neighborhood centered along H Street between 5th and 8th Streets NW. It was settled by Chinese immigrants beginning in the 1930's, but the ethnic population declined rapidly in the 1960's.

The Fortune Cookie

Once, I opened a fortune cookie in a Chinatown
café on H Street only to find it empty. A clam
with no pearl, a magician with nothing up his sleeve.
I made up a fortune that went, "Drink from the well
of life, but beware of the algae." The cookie was
as hard to digest as the improvised fortune.

Once, I met a lawyer who seduced me with words, then
his hands. A smooth-skinned, smooth-talker who made
my ears blush, my stomach do flip-flops. He tried me
on the roof of his DuPont Circle high-rise, found me
innocent. The next morning, I opened a novelty fortune
cookie for breakfast. It said, "Lawyers do it in their briefs."

Once, a fortune in a cookie ripped in two, each
tattered half contained in the cookie's folds.
Carefully, I retrieved the two-part fortune, fit
the pieces together like a jigsaw puzzle. Jagged
cookie quarters lay on the table, uneaten. "You have
a split personality," was what the fortune said.

Once, delirious from hunger, I neglected to tip
the ancient man who delivered egg rolls and shrimp
fried rice to the house on Warren Street. The food
was hot, filling; satisfied my craving. I washed it
down with green tea, stored the leftovers. The fortune
cookie was stale, as difficult to open as a vault.
It said, "Don't press your luck."

KENNETH CARROLL (1959 –)

Kenneth Carroll is the author of a book of poems, *So What! For the White Dude Who Said This Ain't Poetry.* He is the past coordinator of WritersCorps DC and the African American Writers Guild. A US Army Recruitment Office is located at Florida Avenue, where it intersects with Benning Road NE.

Snookie Johnson Goes Down to the Recruiter's Office Near Benning Road & Starts Some Shit

it was right about the time they started drafting for the iraqi war
snookie came to sign up but he didn't walk through the door,

instead he leaped like a madman right through the plate glass
& kicked the recruiting sergeant square in his no-good ass

he said, "i wanna go to the desert, kill some arab chump
& drink his hot blood like water from a barnyard pump

i wanna get bit on my nose by a scorpion wit a bad attitude
i wanna smoke twelve packs a day & eat snake heart for food

i wanna drink poison gas with a side order of sand
& dance with a nuclear missile while digging the junkyard band

i wanna jump in an oil well & get real slick
then have me a party with some them mooslim chicks

cause i'm snookie johnson from a bad neighborhood
& when i get ciced up i don't mean nobody good

so sign me up sergeant & sign me up fast
i'm just raring to kick me some motherfuckin ass"

the sergeant looked at snookie with nothing but disgust
knowing he was the kind of nigga can't nobody trust

"you too damn crazy for the military," the sarge said wit a frown
snookie gave him a sheet of paper & said, "yo man, write dat down."

SAUNDRA ROSE MALEY (1959 -)

Saundra Maley is the co-editor of *A Wild Perfection: The Selected Letters of James Wright,* author of *Solitary Apprenticeship: James Wright and German Poetry*, and co-author of *The Art of the Footnote* and *The Research Guide for the Digital Age.* She teaches at Montgomery College in Takoma Park. The USO (United Service Organizations) was founded in 1941 to coordinate civilian participation in WWII, and ran clubs and canteens in DC. The Willard InterContinental Washington is a luxury hotel located two blocks east of the White House. Famous guests to the hotel have included Abraham Lincoln, Martin Luther King, Jr., P.T. Barnum, Emily Dickinson, Charles Dickens, and Mark Twain.

War Bonds

it was wartime
daisies and maisies in overalls
worked in factories
snapping gum in their teeth
ration spunk
to keep them going

through weekend tours
at the local USO
or late nights
checking hats
for the Willard rooftop garden
it was rough

making ends meet
while their men were at war
in radio worlds
and newspaper print
nights at home were spent reading

letters over and over
like prayers
mouths shaped to the words
and Hershey bars
melted on radiators

SHARAN STRANGE (1959 –)

Sharan Strange is the author of a book of poems, *Ash*, and lived in DC for
seven years before moving to Atlanta to teach at Spelman College. The Route
of the S2 bus runs primarily north to south on 16th Street NW, passing
through the Columbia Heights neighborhood (where it intersects with
Columbia Road NW), to Scott Circle and Lafayette Square.

Saint on the Southbound S2: Ode to a Bus Driver

As if this cross-town journey is a pilgrimage,
you greet Mt. Pleasant's comers with a penitent's stare.
Ataraxic pose despite the jolts, deep-set eyes,
recesses of devotion. Calm brow an altar to

hair thinned enough that you could be taken
for a father. *Padre nuestro* on the southbound S2,
patience in traffic, humility in your cotton jacket,
your simple workman's dinner in a Safeway bag.

The bus fills, empties, and someone here
needs your blessing of small talk of weather and family,
confides in hosannas pooling in your dark irises,
sympathy riding your smile. The woman at Columbia Road

who will go downtown for a third time this week
for pills to save a body whose real joy now is mere motion.
She exits at McPherson, exhorting us to *praise Him*—should we
not also praise you, deliverer without discrimination?

The loud complainers, lovers, babies.
The man who slumbers in his faint perfume
of whiskey and urine. Those of us who give
him room, who see him now—

Surely you know our shortcomings
as you have come to understand
the specificity of misery. Incandescent,
your face gives up its furtive compassion,

a tableau where stubble and blemish are sanctified.
The monotony of stops, the churn of bodies moving past,
all day, the chiming of signals signifying not your release
but others'— There must be burden in this—

Some thank you—yet likely you aren't remembered
in those eddying moments that close the day—
a small gesture in departing,
not quite tribute, much less prayer.

ELIZABETH POLINER (1960 -)

Elizabeth Poliner is the author of a novel-in-stories, *Mutual Life & Casualty*, and her poems have appeared widely in journals such as the *Southern Review, Kenyon Review,* and *Prairie Schooner*. During her twenty years in Washington, DC, she taught creative writing at The Writer's Center, George Washington University, and American University, and now teaches at Hollins University. There are currently 32 community gardens in DC, where residents can sign up for space in shared plots. The gardens are very popular, and most have long waiting lists for new members.

Students Painting in the Community Garden on Newark Street

Standing scattered
as seeds, planted
at easels,

their heads rise
above the cosmos,
zinnias, and marigolds,

which, freed
of any gardener's intent,
have burst

into tall, tangled
October overgrowth.
Scarecrows—

still and upright,
arms lifted at strange angles—
they hang,

hang,
patient in this hushed
wild field.

ESTHER IVEREM (1960 -)

Esther Iverem is the author of two books of poems, *The Time: A Portrait of a Journey Home*, and *Living in Babylon*, and a book of film criticism, *We Gotta Have It: Twenty Years of Seeing Black at the Movies, 1986-2006*. She is the founder of SeeingBlack.com. She writes here in protest of the second inauguration of President George W. Bush, commenting in particular on the increased security in a post-9-11 city. The poem is also a pointed reminder of how national events are so often local events as well for DC residents.

Second Inauguration

How high and sharp the rooftop snipers.
How empty and fearful the downtown streets.
How many rows deep the local police.
How many rows deep the bussed in police.
How many rows deep the National Guard.
How many rows deep the soldiers.
How many rows deep the secret service.
How many rows deep the service that is no secret.

In D.C.'s windswept cold, service to the beast
Is the easiest job to find, the easiest way to die,
The easiest way to kill, the easiest way to
Silence protesters held behind fences,

Barricades and bleachers
With marvelous puppets and placards that say,
"No more! No more! No More Blood for Oil!"
Or for Bechtel, Lockheed Martin, Halliburton,
The Carlyle Group, Aegis, or Bearing Point.

How cordoned off the streets
Filled with bomb-sniffing dogs.
The usual spot for the silver hot dog truck
And F.B.I. tourist t-shirts now
A command center for thick men in trench coats
Wearing sunglasses and wires coiling from their ears.

How sleek the Cadillac limousine.
How direct the flight of an orange
Before it goes thonk on the limousine's side.
How quickly the coated, shielded and fed men
Speed up the limo, and run along side it
—armed parade attendants for a bullet-proof float.
How furry the mink coat-wearing fans.
How cold and pink their faces, with puffs
Of hot air rising from their lips like car exhaust.
How smartly the commander-in-chief
Climbs from the limo, and walks along the empty streets,
Waving to empty bleachers, empty faces, and cold empty air.

How alien is the little commander standing at the podium,
Declaring himself God's messenger, and to be doing God's will
Backed by the rooftop snipers, the local police,
The bussed in police, the National Guard, the soldiers,
The secret police, and the common service that is no secret.

How high up is God looking down on this moment?
And how quickly is the earth warming?
How quickly gathering the patchwork quilt of death.
The bullets and cutting, the rapes and electric shocks.
How quickly stacking and reeking the corpses.
How trap-door shut the minds, how trap-door shut the eyes.
In this new Reich of soldiers, silicone living and satellite death.

How high and sharp the rooftop snipers.
How empty and fearful the downtown streets.

How many rows deep the local police.
How many rows deep the bussed in police.
How many rows deep the National Guard.
How many rows deep the soldiers.
How many rows deep the secret service.
How many rows deep the service that is no secret.

RANDALL HORTON (1961 -)

Randall Horton is the author of two books of poems, *The Lingua Franca of Ninth Street,* and *The Definition of Place*, and editor of *Reverie: Midwest African American Literature,* and the anthology *Fingernails Across the Chalkboard: Poetry and Prose on HIV/AIDS from the Black Diaspora.* Marvin Gaye was born and raised in southeast DC, and did his first performances with The Moonglows before moving to Detroit to sign with Motown Records. The "hollowed buildings" of 14th Street were the result of four days of riots following the assassination of Martin Luther King, Jr. in April 1968. Businesses along 14th Street were looted and burned; the neighborhood did not recover economically until the 1990's.

Marvin Gaye Sings the National Anthem at the NBA All-Star Game

Life should be so easy as a boy
        on swing set thrusting both feet forward, pulling
            his face through a breeze, or

to be curled in a lover's arm listening to river swirls'
        meditation. War rages against
            this lean silk in the spotlight.

Oh how to articulate the madness except
        through a drum machine, distant family member
            to the djembe—

an electronic beat tingles the ear hole.
        Now layer sensation with voice smooth
            as hot silver flowing into half-dollars,

brighter than a thousand camera flashes,
        & the mirrored shades gleaming
                is for others to reflect themselves.

Oh the fork tongue whispering
        knows the five-spots festering Southeast DC, has seen
                14th Street's hollowed buildings

in a state of rigor-mortis from the 60's: a construct
        of crumbling brick structures
                held by aging plyboard.

A moon of narcotic drains slowly from the nostrils, everything
        bone bright—numb
                as if this may be the apocalypse.

Oh they have chosen a troubled man
        to signify Old Glory, which unfurls
                if nothing but faithfully.

CHRISTINA DAUB (1961 -)

Christina Daub founded *The Plum Review* and the Plum Writers Retreat. She has taught creative writing at George Washington University, The Writer's Center, and in both Maryland and Virginia's poets-in-the-schools programs. The Washington Metropolitan Transit Authority broke ground for its first underground trains in 1969, and began operating in 1976. Stations were designed by architect Harry Weese, with vaulted ceilings made from poured concrete.

In the Metro

The wind is my mother
rushing from the deep tunnel.
Relax, I tell her.
I know you're there.

For a long time
I did not want to think of her,
though the bird bones of her wrists
inhabit mine, the flyaway hair.

Somehow, the dead never leave us.
They just recirculate as air
or light or shadow. Or in the slow
monologue of my youngest son.

I take his hand to board the train.
He speaks whole worlds to me.
Somehow he knows her words.
This time I listen.

BRIAN GILMORE 1962 -)

Brian Gilmore is a public interest attorney and the author of two books of poems, *Elvis Presley is Alive and Well and Living in Harlem*, and *Jungle Nights & Soda Fountain Rags*. His poem is written in tribute to Gaston Neal, who moved to DC in the late 1950's and became a leader in the Black Arts Movement. Neal founded the New School of Afro-American Thought in1966, and by the early 1990's was a much-sought-after "underground legend" on the DC poetry scene. Neal died in DC in 1999.

billy eckstine comes to washington, d.c.

for gaston neal

he strolled in
w/ amiri baraka

decked out in
a long dark
trench coat
yassar arafat
scarf

beret

made me think of
dali
black panthers

only he wasn't no painter
because he wasn't smiling like
romare bearden

and wasn't no panther
so i was told
but

    he was carrying
    poems and
    the people
    were his politics

a friend nudged me
told me he was good
maybe he might
read a few
after baraka
but he didn't
because we wasn't
that blessed
yet
wasn't time for

"mumbo sauce please!

  mumbo sauce please!"

dripping thick over deep
fried chicken wings
served w/o napkins

i met him years later
he told me
about my city
how he was there
on 14th street
when "murder one"
left junkies laid out
in alleys with needles
in arms
soaring like
baseballs over
banneker playground
fence

he told me he talked to
langston hughes over the phone
langston treated him like
they had known each other
for 49 years
like they had grown
up together in
joplin missouri

back in the day he was there
on u street with stokely when
word came that the king was dead
and the country would burn
break crack and wail

sometimes i look at him
see my grandfather
on the porch preaching
about unions
or willie "the lion" smith
at the piano
reminding young upstarts
that his fingers can
still dance like
chorus girls
rehearsing for
a show

other times i look at him
my friends and i are sharing
cold beer
bragging about dunking
reverse lay ups
pool games
we no longer have time
to play

    i finally did hear
    his poetry
    now i know why
    pennsylvania steel towners
    need other neighborhoods to love

down the lazy river to rebel w/
the rest
fight off "the horse"
like jack johnson running from
the mann act
shaking it loose from his body
until the horse finds
weaker souls

no more rides on the horse these days
this body ain't no amusement park

pittsburgh headed
to washington d.c. to
write some songs

like billy eckstine
coming here a second life
is lived

but don't call this
no dickens tale

ELIZABETH ALEXANDER (1962 –)

Elizabeth Alexander was born in New York and raised in DC, and now serves
as chair of the African American Studies Program at Yale University. Her
five books of poems include *The Venus Hottentot, Antebellum Dream Book*,
and a collection for young adults co-authored with Marilyn Nelson, *Miss
Crandall's School for Young Ladies and Little Misses of Color.* Alexander
was invited to read her poem, "Praise Song for the Day," at the inauguration
of President Barack Obama in 2009. The Knickerbocker Theater, which
once sat at the corner of 18th Street and Columbia Avenue NW in the Adams
Morgan neighborhood, was the site of DC's worst snow disaster, in which
the theater's roof collapsed in 1922, killing 98 and injuring 133. The collapse
took place during a screening of the movie, "Get-Rich-Quick Wallingford."

Early Cinema

According to Mister Hedges, the custodian
who called upon their parents

According to Mister Hedges, the custodian
who called upon their parents
after young Otwiner and young Julia
were spotted at the matinee
of Rudolph Valentino in The Sheik
at the segregated Knickerbocker Theater
in the uncommon Washington December
of 1922, "Your young ladies
were misrepresenting themselves today,"
meaning, of course, that they were passing.
After coffee and no cake were finished
and Mister Hedges had buttoned his coat
against the strange evening chill,
choice words were had with Otwiner and Julia,
shame upon the family, shame upon the race.

How they'd longed to see Rudolph Valentino,
who was swarthy like a Negro, like the finest Negro man.
In The Sheik, they'd heard, he was turbaned,
whisked damsels away in a desert cloud.
They'd heard this from Lucille and Ella
who'd put on their fine frocks and French,
claiming to be "of foreign extraction"
to sneak into the Knickerbocker Theater
past the usher who knew their parents
but did not know them.
They'd heard this from Mignon and Doris
who'd painted carmine bindis on their foreheads
braided their black hair tight down the back,
and huffed, "We'll have to take this up with the Embassy"
to the squinting ticket taker.
Otwiner and Julia were tired of Oscar Michaux,
tired of church, tired of responsibility,
rectitude, posture, grooming, modulation,
tired of homilies each way they turned,
tired of colored right and wrong.
They wanted to be whisked away.

The morning after Mister Hedges' visit
the paperboy cried "Extra!" and Papas
shrugged camel's hair topcoats over pressed pajamas
and Mamas read aloud at the breakfast table,

"No Colored Killed When Roof Caves In"
at the Knickerbocker Theater
at the evening show
from a surfeit of snow on the roof.
One hundred others dead.

It appeared that God had spoken.
There was no school that day,
no movies for months after.

JOEL DIAS-PORTER (1962 -)

Joel Dias-Porter is a National Poetry Slam champion, and editor of the poetry anthology *The Black Rooster Social Inn*. He has a CD of jazz and poetry, *LibationSong*. Dias-Porter served in the US Air Force before moving to DC. The main part of the Vietnam Memorial was designed by Maya Lin and completed in 1982. The black granite walls are inscribed with the names of all soldiers killed or missing in action from the war.

Hush Now, Don't Explain

(for Rob)

Under a sapphire ceiling
the three of us walk west
on Constitution Ave.
At 19th St. we become
black threads weaving
through a quilt of white tourists.
You and Denise ask me
what I remember of the war.
I recall in black and white,
helicopters swarming like locusts,
two men emerging from a jungle
bearing a bandaged comrade.
A Buddhist monk wrapped in robes
a warmer orange than
the flames which engulfed him.
I was barely old enough
to understand the flame's finality.
Our conversation fades as
we approach the book of names.
It says Robert Louis Howard,

Panel 22W.
You say Thua Thien, June 1969.
We round the corner,
find the headstone of an era,
an eternal funeral.
Who knows if the sudden quiet
is reverence or shame.
Roses, wreaths and carnations,
bright as fresh blood
lean against the stone,
heads bowed.
A legless vet rolls by,
the eye of his camera blinking furiously.
The name sits
thirteen lines from the top.
The tallest, I'm drafted to make the trace.
I square the paper
shading to reveal a shade.
As I hand you the ghost of a name,
the arithmetic hits me.
The summer of '69
found you in diapers.
All you've had for a Dad
is a folded flag,
and a Sergeant's smile
on a curling Polaroid.
Slowly, the reflecting pools
of our eyes fill.
Trembling, you clutch the letter
that vexes still. Why?
We walk to the benches
trailing teardrops.
Denise hums a balm
as we huddle and rock.
Hush now.
Below us, three tight-lipped
bronze soldiers.
Above us, a flag spilling
like blood down a bayonet.
Above that, an August sky
almost blue
as the tremor
in Denise's contralto.

CARLEASA COATES (1962 -)

Carleasa Coates is a trial attorney whose poems have been awarded Cave Canem and Soul Mountain Fellowships. Independence Avenue SW is a major road that runs along the south side of the National Mall.

The Woman at the End of Independence

In twenty two degree weather,
at the crossing near the Potomac river,

the woman in the red coat holds
a help me I'm homeless sign.

Her eyes wrinkle around the edges.
Her tattered muffler hides teeth missing.

I've seen her here before. Guarding
our mergings, our comings, our busyness.

She is the tug out of the heat
of my life. The wonder where she sleeps at night.

She is the poor I never want to face.
She is my sixth grade teacher gone mad.

The woman punched behind the wall.
She is us wading waist deep in despair.

She is the stop I need.
The blast to my cold indifference.

ROD SMITH (1962 -)

Rod Smith is the author of eleven books of poems, including *Deed, The Good House,* and *In Memory of My Theories*, and co-editor of *The Selected Letters of Robert Creeley*. He edits *Aerial Magazine*, publishes Edge Books, and manages Bridge Street Bookstore. Smith is known for his use of experimental forms, including flarf, a type of found poetry that mines the internet for phrases that are arranged into poems. In this poem, Smith appropriates the language of tourism, a major DC industry.

Washington, DC is Great!

for Ara Shirinyan

Washington, DC is a city that routinely appears in the news week after week.

The westernmost point of the Great Inverted Pentagram
of Washington DC is George Washington Circle Park.

My family and I recently visited your amazing city for the first time,
and may I say it was a great experience.

DC is a great city full of history and culture
that becomes home to a large number of UVA alumni.

If you are looking for great cheap eats, then Washington DC is a great
place to be.

Bike tours are a great way to explore D.C. There
are also many phamacy jobs in Washington, DC.

We've got great tickets to all kinds of musicals and plays this year.

Visit the neighborhood surrounding Georgetown University for great
shopping from designer boutiques.

I love Washington, DC and it thrills me that this type of Washington,
DC is available.

GREAT NEWS FROM WASHINGTON DC!

A great nation deserves the truth.

Washington DC is a wonderful place to be in the Summer and you can find
an enormous amount of great deals throughout the city.

It's almost worth not getting blind drunk on Friday nights so you can be
up early enough to hit the Arlington Farmer's Market on Saturday.

My son and I had never been to Washington DC. We took your tour
this past weekend and it was a great!

Once upon a time in Washington, DC, there gathered over two hundred Aggies, desperate for some good food.

Washington, DC is a great furnished place with lots of malls.

Washington DC. WOW!

Very well done, I can see you had a fantastic trip in America!
It was on Rachel Ray $40 a Day show.

Great Washington D.C. restaurants, great shopping and a contemporary mix of American people can be found strolling the city streets of an area.

You Can Even Take a Woman to on a Date in Washington DC.

Another great new option that Dish TV Washington Navy Yard Washington DC provides for its subscribers is portable programming through its new PocketDish.

DC is great and way too much to see there for just one.

The home page of James Trotta's site for vacation/trip itineraries features some
great ideas for a trip to Washington DC. Uncork the Wine, Uncork the Flavor, Uncork the Fun.

Great Wraps & Cheesesteaks, Union Station, Washington, DC—poor customer service experience.

Washington, D.C., and Northern Virginia: Great Destinations.

SARAH BROWNING (1962 -)

Sarah Browning is the author of a book of poems, *Whiskey in the Garden of Eden*, and founder of DC Poets Against the War and Split This Rock Poetry Festival. She describes Lincoln's journey from his "Summer White House" at the Armed Forces Retirement Home (popularly known as the Soldier's Home), down what was then the Seventh Street Pike (now Georgia Ave. NW). Lincoln and his family slept in a cottage on the grounds in 1862, 1863, and 1864, seeking out one of the city's highest elevations during the hottest months. Father north on Georgia Avenue, the Walter Reed Army Medical Center has been the major rehabilitation hospital for wounded soldiers returning from current conflicts in Iraq and Afghanistan.

The Fifth Fact

For Ben's project he must research five facts
about his African-American hero and write them
on posterboard. He chooses Harriet Tubman,
whose five facts are: *Her father's name was Ben.*
Her mother's name was Old Rit. She was born
in 1820 and died in 1913. She was born in Maryland
and died in New York. Ben asks for advice
about his fifth fact and I suggest: *She led more than*
300 people to freedom. Ben sighs the way he does
now and says, *Everyone knows that, Mom.*

So I try to remember the book we read yesterday,
search for the perfect fact, the one that will match
his four facts and satisfy his almost-seven mind.
Remember, I ask, *she was a spy for the North*
during the Civil War? It's a hit! He writes it:
Harriet Tubman was a spy for the north during
the civil war. It was a war between the north
which is where the slaves were trying to get
and the south which is where they were.
Before the war, Abraham Lincoln signed a form
that said All the slaves everywhere are free!
which is one of the reasons they were fighting.

On summer mornings, Lincoln rode his horse
to work down the Seventh Street Turnpike
close to my new home. Down Georgia Avenue
past The Hunger Stopper and Pay Day 2 Go and liquor
stores and liquor stores. Past Cluck-U-Chicken
and Fish in the 'Hood and Top Twins Faze II
Authentic African Cuisine and the newish Metro station
and all those possibilities gleaming in developers' eyes.

There goes Lincoln's horse down Georgia Avenue
from the Soldier's Home to the White House—
much cooler up here in the country, in the neighborhood,
at the hospital. And there's Walt Whitman, the sworn poet
of every dauntless rebel the world over, hanging around
his street corner every morning to bow to the president
at Thomas Circle by the homeless guys. It's 100 years now
since any president summered at the Soldier's Home.
But I was born only 50 years after Harriet Tubman died,
all these centuries we drag into the next century and the next.

Writing here, in my new neighborhood, the city old
and new around me, I see Harriet Tubman
and Lincoln and Uncle Walt and the true stories
and sometimes our own despair like Washington's
summer malaria, her 40 war hospitals, Whitman moving
from bed to bed, stroking the hair of so many dying boys.

North up Georgia Avenue in our own soldiers' home –
Walter Reed – the boys and now girls too
mourn the ghosts of their own legs and arms
and our capacity for love. Where is their
sworn poet? Harriet Tubman born
so close. All these heroes under our feet.

JOSHUA WEINER (1963 -)

Joshua Weiner is the author of two books of poems, *The World's Room* and
From the Book of Giants. He teaches at the University of Maryland and
serves as poetry editor of *Tikkun*. This poem is set on the White House's
South Lawn, which faces the Ellipse and the National Mall. The South Lawn
is the site of State Arrival Ceremonies, the annual Egg Rolling Contest, the
Rose Garden, and is where Marine One, the presidential helicopter, lands.
Camden Yards is the official ballpark of the Baltimore Orioles, and Cal
Ripken was their star shortstop until his retirement in 2001.

National Pastime
(Washington D.C., 2002)

Late spring evenings at the neighborhood diamond,
the light a mellow custard before the bugs come out,

extra dads walk the outfield spotting for glass and dog shit,
anticipating season's end with each spill of Gatorade.
When the league director shows up with a surprise invitation,
who can believe it: Eli's team to play the South Lawn,
inexplicably, with the worst record in the league; until
a parent points out later, "He's courting the Spanish vote,"
the District's one bilingual school, pitching logic into relief.
The parents mostly Democrats, labor lawyers, journalists,
the coach a Mid-East peace negotiator, explicably
out of work—should we boycott, or protest somehow
the children's fairy tale finale? Should our
censure ruin the six-year olds'
requested appearance at the White House?—Conviction
competing with conviction, we hear
our cameras calling to be fingered from their sleep.

Game day, fresh Cardinal duds throw glow
on expectant faces, the new world order here a batting roster.
Players take positions, charmed by the announcer's melody
massaging the mind as if in Camden Yards.
Bush sweats with pleasure, Big Kid among the kids,
with Tom Ridge coaching first, his designated
radio curling like an ear inside his ear;
Mayor Williams coaches third, his bemused stoic posture
resigned to the symbolic placement;
and the Orioles mascot works
the parents in the stand, the staffers, and special invites—
families of the most recent
publicly acknowledged Pentagon dead.

Mercifully, one inning, two photo ops, and a picnic.
A White House reporter approaches Eli for an interview;
the tape recorder insinuating official history,
the boy's back straightens as if tied to puppet strings.
"If you were putting together a team
and you had to choose between President Bush
and Cal Ripken, who would you choose?"
Eli thinks a moment, shrugging off expectations.
"Cal Ripken," he throws back.
"And why is that?"—the newsman's glove is ready.
"He's a real baseball player." (Pitching logic into relief).

Laid out under shade, on grass plush as any carpet,
I watch the team of marksmen camouflaged in foliage along the fence,

binoculars searching the streets while the House music spins
—is this possible?—Wild Cherry, 1976,

"I tried to understand this /
I thought they were out of their minds /
How could I be so foolish / To not see
I was the one behind"—behind the fence,
inside the game, America's favorite
pastime, America's number one show, streaming back through
the bicentennial Tomahawk testing Legionnaire's disease,
Israel to Ford: Send in the Clowns Saul Bellow Rocky All
the President's Men, as the New York Yankees
take Entebbe, Pol Pot makes use of the Steadicam
and the Supreme Court, after great deliberation, rules that
Robert Lowell's Selected Poems is neither inherently cruel nor unusual,
though Richard Leakey's discovery falls
outside their jurisdiction: a skull of homo erectus from 1.5 million years ago;
and when he lifts it to his ear like a transistor radio
it sings to him the song I hear "losing every step by the way,"
snaking through Tom Ridge's wire, the soundtrack
to Colin Powell's tears, "burnin' down
the night stands" of President Bush's brain—

And just when / it hit me / somebody turned around
and shouted / 'Play that funky music, white boy, /
Play that funky music right / Play that funky music,
white boy / Lay down that boogie, and play
that funky music till you die /
Till you die / Oh, till
you die'"

—deciduous giants of the South Lawn stretching out their arms,
leaves whispering frantically to an empty blue sky . . .

THOMAS SAYERS ELLIS (1963 -)

Thomas Sayers Ellis is a native of DC and author of two books of poems, *The Maverick Room* and *The Genuine Negro Hero*. He teaches at Sarah Lawrence College and Leslie University. Originally settled by freed slaves after the Civil War, Barry Farms is a neighborhood in southeast DC, adjacent to St. Elizabeth's Hospital, consisting almost entirely of public housing.

Tambourine Tommy

More man
Than myth, more myth
Than freak, he would come out
Between bands

In a harness of bells
And high-waters
Held together and up
By a belt of rope.

His skin was thick
As friendship, his spot-lit scalp
Clean as the repaired dome
Of the U.S. Capitol.

Rickety raw
And rickety strong,
He'd run from Barry Farms
To Mount Vernon

With bricks
Borrowed from the wall
Around St. Elizabeth's Hospital
In each hand.

There was struggle
In his dance,
Like first-of-the-month
Or Election Day downtown.

His arms tried to
Free Terrance Johnson,
His trickster legs
Rayful Edmond

But such drama
Never made him more
Than spectacle or more
Than beast.

No one thought
Of him as artist,
No one thought
Of him as activist.

His craft, the way
He beat himself
(head, shoulders, knees
and toes), proved he

Was one of us,
A soul searcher
Born and raised
In the District,

Proved he
Could reach in,
Blend, ease before entering,
Proved he

Was our phoenix,
Nobody's Stonestreet,
Part hustler, part athlete,
Tougher than all of Southeast.

NAOMI AYALA (1964 –)

Naomi Ayala is the author of two books of poems, *Wild Animals on the Moon* and *This Side of Early*. A native of Puerto Rico, she resides in DC, where she serves as the Executive Director of the Capitol Letters Writing Center. She describes a restaurant in the Adams Morgan neighborhood, where a large percentage of the city's Latino population lives.

Restaurante Santa Rosa

a Vanessa Bustos

En los últimos doce días
el sol no ha pasado

En los últimos doce días
el sol no ha pasado
por los cristales de Santa Rosa
y nadie se ríe como nos reíamos antes.
La radiola está ensimismada,
el pulpo frío, las mazorcas de maíz
en su ensueño de verano.
Algunos hombres se dan cervezas
solos y fuman
uno reniega el embarazo de su novia
arando días que guardan secretos.
Y una mujer quiere cambiarse el nombre
a murmullo, a ola, a viento.
Las plantas plásticas se ríen del clorofilo,
le tiran besitos al cielo encancáranublado.
Tres encendedores se encienden de una vez
cerca del salero
a quien le pesan tantos granitos de arroz.
Y cómo pasan los peatones afuera
tan lejos de aquí y tan cerca
sin pensar en el cielo, quien
queriendo cambiar de historia
se acuesta a morir entre nosotros.

Santa Rosa Restaurant

for Vanessa Bustos

In the last twelve days
the sun has not come through
the windowpanes of Santa Rosa,
and no one laughs the way we used to.
The jukebox is engrossed in her thoughts,
the octopus and cobs of corn
in their daydream of summer.
Some men drink their beers
alone and smoke
one renounces his lover's pregnancy
furrowing in days of well kept secrets.
And a woman wants to change her name
to whisper, wave, wind.
The plastic plants mock chlorophyll,
blow little kisses to the overcast sky.

Three cigarette lighters spark up at once
near a salt shaker
whose tiny grains of rice weigh him down.
And how pedestrians pass by outside
☐so far from here and so close,
without a thought about the sky, who
wanting to change his history,
lies down to die among us.

ALAN SPEARS (1964 -)

Alan Spears, a life-long DC resident, has published poems in *Potomac Review,
Gargoyle, Innisfree Poetry Journal,* and *Beltway Poetry Quarterly.* This
poem speaks of two kinds of lead exposure: from bullets, and from tap water,
the latter referring to a water treatment problem the city experienced in the
late 1990's.

It's Amazing What You Get Used To

I call them "morons."
A group of guys
most likely young, stupid-ass brothers
that have been driving by
the neighborhood the last few nights
shooting up the abandoned gas station on the corner.
I've never seen them
but I know their work
by the fury of their assault
and the sound of screeching car tires
as they speed away.

What's worse than the bullets
is the dead silence afterwards.
No cops, no sirens wailing to the rescue.
No neighbors stepping out
to consult with one another in hushed, worried tones.
Nothing.

When the "morons" struck this morning
they roused me from a sound sleep.
It took a few seconds to realize
they were at it again,
as the closer we get to summer the more

folks 'round here break out leftover firecrackers and M-80's...
But these were bullets
and before I could catch myself,
in a moment of soporific optimism
I reached over to adjust the wicker partition that serves as my curtain,
a pathetic "just in case" to protect against stray bullets.
The shots rang
the tires screeched
and then...
Nothing all over again.

I lay there in the humid silence...
Thinking about all the other people in the neighborhood
angry, afraid, and muted just like me.

After a few minutes I rolled out of bed
and went downstairs for a glass of water.
DC tap.
It tasted a lot less like lead than usual.
For which I was truly grateful.

RAMOLA D (1964 -)

Ramola D is the author of a collection of short fiction, *Temporary Lives*, and a book of poems, *Invisible Season*. She teaches at The Writer's Center. The Metro system serves DC and surrounding communities. It opened in 1976 and is the second-busiest rapid transit system in the US (in number of passenger trips), after New York.

I Saw Her Rise

The woman rose from the twilit well,
            dark, the well
                    of stairs from the metro,
                        in her hand
the shuddering and open mouths
        of white arrested flowers, long
                stems and waxed engulfing leaves
    framed

                            against the earth

and tinsel flick of pink in the pot
        she held, I saw her rise, the lilies
            white about her clothes
and shoulder pushed
        up against her face, her body pressed
            into the substance of that white
restraint and edge
        of yellow, faintest orange, tiger
            stripe

                  her body leaning
forward into
        that stemmed chaos of lilies,
        her body working furiously
        at arrival. And I saw her lives
cascade
        inside her hands, the ones that held
            the echo of her longing, choate, formed
            inside the throats of lilies: blue
            cup on a sill, shower of rain, hint
of marriage in her mouth
and its break
        inside her eyes, somewhere a child
            falling through her body
            into the world: its survival
in her space
among, between, around
        the selves she must have etched
        carefully into birth: known, watched over,
        loved, and the selves
she still attempts
to resist:
        their pale insistent hands
        clustering, their faces—like
souls themselves, transparent, wistful—I
saw her rise
        and hurry forward
        into her future of sudden
        possibility: thick skies and rain
        among the still, the unresisting trees,
            light
a rake, gold and flicker, stark

shudder of light
low against the trees, streaming blind
in descent against her breath,
light
in lapse and rise
inside that hollow choir
of petals, carousel
of light, her face
still throned
inside the dusk and violet
of the stairwell's night, hastening, turned,
the lilies trembling, alive—
I saw her rise.

KATHI MORRISON-TAYLOR (1965 -)

Kathi Morrison-Taylor is the author of a book of poems, *By the Nest*, co-director of the Joaquin Miller Cabin Reading Series in Rock Creek Park, and teaches English as a Second Language in Fairfax County, VA. After the terrorist attacks of September 11, 2001, security increased in DC, and Reagan Washington National Airport was closed for several weeks, making downtown areas noticeably quieter. The US Department of Homeland Security was formed in 2003 in response to the attacks.

Bomb Pop

In downtown Washington
just blocks from the White House
you can still buy a Bomb Pop—
its red, white, and blue
warhead portrait displayed
on the Good Humor cart
next to Fudgsicles and Sundae Cones;
its novelty rocket of cherry,
lemon and raspberry
a bestseller in this no-fly zone.

Last Friday, a bomb threat
cleared the monuments,
closed Constitution
and Independence for hours.

Trapped on the mall, a tourist dad
stopped to cool off with a Bomb Pop,
licked those memories—
Cold War, fallout shelters,
brain freeze—basking
in Homeland Security.

Forgive me, but I suspect
someone's filming me
as I ask for one,
as I'm pointing,
as the vendor's reaching
into his silo.

Francisco Aragón (1965 -)

Francisco Aragón is the author of four books of poems, including *Puerta del Sol* and *Glow of Our Sweat*, and editor of the anthology *The Wind Shifts: New Latino Poetry*. He works in DC, where he directs Letras Latinas, the literary program of the Institute for Latino Studies at Notre Dame University. This poem was written as a direct address to President George W. Bush.

To the President

after Rubén Darío

Should I quote the good
book you claim to know;

or perhaps our late bearded
bard—might these be ways

of reaching you? Primitive
modern, simple complex—

one part wily astute
animal, three parts owner

of a ranch: conglomeration
is what you are, poised

for another incursion.
Lean, strong specimen

of your breed, polite you
hardly read when not

in a saddle, or spreading manure.
You see a building in flames

as vital, progress a spewing
volcano. And where you point

and place your bullet
you stake the future—yours

and ours. And so:
not so fast. O there's

no doubting the heft
of this nation: it moves it

shifts—a tremor travels
down to the tip

of the continent; you raise
your voice and it's

bellowing we hear (The sky
is mine), stars in the east

sun in the west. People
are clothes, their cars,

Sunday attire at church,
a harbor lady lighting

the journey with a torch.
But America, sir,

is North, Central,
and South—delicate

wing of a beetle,
thundering sheet

of water (our cubs
are crossing

over). And though,
O man of bluest eye,

you believe your truth,
it is not—you are not

the world.

TONY MEDINA (1966 -)

Tony Medina is the author of twelve poetry books for adults and children, including *Committed to Breathing*, and *My Old Man Was Always on the Lam*, and co-editor of three poetry anthologies, including *Bum Rush the Page: A Def Poetry Jam*. He is an Associate Professor of Creative Writing at Howard University. Café Nema is a restaurant on U Street NW, in the heart of the historic district that Pearl Bailey once called the "Black Broadway."

Cannibals On U Street

for The Young Lions at Café Nema

Regardless of which nightstick
Hits you upside your head
It still cracks in 4-4 time

The streets still flow red
The gutter chokes on cherry blossoms
Rain splinters into kisses

Horses gallop out of horns
Punching holes through
Smoky neon air

Death is a woman
You mistook for a bass
Stringing her along

Somewhere a bomb is dropping
Somewhere a baby is screaming
Somewhere your mama is dreaming

You'll come home
You'll come home

Dan Vera (1967 –)

Dan Vera is the author of a book of poems, *The Space Between Our Danger and Delight,* and co-editor of Vrzhu Press. With Michael Gushue, he co-curates the monthly Brookland Reading Series. The area around Georgia Avenue and Harvard Street, just north of Howard University, is home to several Afrocentric stores.

Ode to the Black Nationalist Pharaoh Head of Georgia Avenue

Oh how we have need of you
Black Nationalist Pharaoh Head of Georgia Avenue.

How we have need of your proud scowl gazing down
on Harvard Street as we make our way home each day.

Here among European diasporic architecture,
colonial, deco, craftsman, rowhouse,
you lorded over the mild and the meek,
handsome in your headdress, reminding your people
of their roots in a land of historic geometries.

No scepter or servants,
just that head jutting out
from the Black Nationalist bookshop
where my friend once entered,
and being told it was only for blacks,
asked, "How do you know that I'm not?"

Oh, Black Nationalist Pharaoh Head of Georgia Avenue,
who took you down when they closed up the bookshop?
Where did they cart you to, Black Nationalist Pharaoh Head?
What avenues do you gaze down upon now?
What message do you impart to the hungering crowds?

I imagine you now in Africa,
in the Kush, rubbing elbows with other Pharaoh heads,
gazing upon your pyramids again.

The empty wall here calls for you.
For we still have need of you
Black Nationalist Pharaoh Head of Georgia Avenue.
Your gaze is still needed.

DANIEL GUTSTEIN (1968 -)

Daniel Gutstein writes poetry and fiction, and works at the Maryland Institute College of Art, where he runs the Writing Studio and Learning Resource Center, and teaches creative writing. This poem travels from the Baltimore-Washington International Thurgood Marshall Airport in Linthicum, MD, on the commuter rail line (MARC) to Union Station, the MARC terminus and the grand ceremonial train station located on Capitol Hill.

Valise variations

in the licorice chew
of girl's reflection
rainy window on commuter rail
at dayfall
wet street perpendicular to
the nowhere of streetlamp's sickly hood
beat of wet wind
beat of strobes guiding aircraft
toward baltimore / washington
in the shoulder to shoulder
of traveler valise
missing
your pretty teeth
i could anger simply or collapse
cuss of transmission wire
slush of underpass

*

time is a grid of latitudes
and darkenings
time is a grid of plurals

*

light fails on doublefile track
scrawny spraypaint diss
leaner against standpipe fails
buddies in half-cammy slouch
billboard platitude
world of haste fails   ·
twisty scrapyard
elbow of steamshovel
bioengine of archway fails
neon powerball total
revivitization or
momentum fails
signal and switchbox and torque
spasm of brake and guzz of electrics

                    *

what arrives is percussion
shoe / dank
shoe / dank
what is mass ave & 3rd st
union station's dome of exhaust
little and less
sole / scuff
what is percussion

                    *

hashes a scoop of cranberry
a scoop of taters
a scoop of stuffing
outside public kitchen
a mimic thrasher
catbird
building nest and nestling
atop crown of flickery signage "Eats
in the measure of its eye
its rustic housecoat
missing
the weather of your wit
kind instrument of your variance

                    *

i kindle the closet bulb
throw an arm of your nightgown
around a shirtcollar
tipsy fond
garments on their hangers
renewing the likes of our bodies

*

time is a grid of latitudes

Toni Asante Lightfoot (1968 -)

Toni Asante Lightfoot is a DC native who founded the first spoken word reading series in DC, at It's Your Mug in Georgetown, and is co-founder of the Modern Urban Griots. She has been Artistic Director of Blackout Arts Collective in Boston, and Director of the T.E.A.C.H. program at Young Chicago Authors. The Capital Center (also known briefly as the US Airways Arena) was located in Mitchellville, MD from 1973 to 1997; it was a major sports and concert venue.

Mothership Future Dream Palabramorphetic

Blue haze floats and grows over the roof of the Capital
        Center. This place is new, shiny,   unprepared.
        There are a dozen Black folk on stage dressed
        psychoafronegrofuturmetastylistic.

Flue must be clogged, smoke unable to rise out
        tumbles down. My sister is bellbottoms, braids,
        and anticipation. Me? 10 year old cock blocking
        machine revved with starsky & hutch lunchbox.

Flee my mind and shwuzzle into the seat. World
        conjugates every word as they primpoon around me.
        Who needs a dictionary when more precise conjectures
        are unfolding with each drum-horn progression.

Fled my home tonight. Any night away is a dream.
        Who knows when the next flurry of meaness will fly
        from brother to brother,   sister to mother.
        When fathers escape   those left standing   crumble.

Sled down the flurries of funk fritters dolking in my chest.
        Then I noticed the stage flit-flut with the most delic dancing bird
        ever feathered. No cage holds her. She chooses who will stroke her.
        Behold Goddess! Smite any bars on which she beats her wing.

Seed of wild fruit sows into my pituitary producing fragrant funkmoans.
        Skunky sunshine slips under my eyelids. When closed
        groove monsters morph into cartoons no network is genius enough
        to play. Daffy is sunday school. Dr. Funkenstien is Church

sending you on a sweet chariot ride. The worshifters flimmer
        the surface of space and at its edge the crowd drimmkels
        with gyroscope song. Where do these images orgynate?
        What Malcolm prophecy revealed this? Let me rise and

fend off the man who's now sitting next to my ward.
        The warden will want details and I've already lost
        too many memories to sleep. I wake up 13 times on 13 different
        planets. My sister and me whisping free on all of them.

Fund alien artistians is on the picket sign I don in front
        of the Black House. George Clinton sits on the steps
        with some weed and crème brulee. Informing us he
        gave up and joined the clan. We break the barriers.

Funk strikes and burns the masquerade off my parents.
        All crispy they beg my forgiveness. I blessticate them
        with funk's power, the glory. The mothership
        comes. I dream my sister remembers all of this.

KWAME ALEXANDER (1968 -)

Kwame Alexander is the author of 13 books, including *And Then You Know: New and Selected Poems* He produces the annual Capital BookFest, and is founding director of the literacy program Book-in-a-Day, and in the 1990's was editor and publisher of BlackWords Books. The U Street corridor, part of the Shaw neighborhood, is home to numerous restaurants, shopping boutiques, theaters, and clubs. The neighborhood suffered a long economic decline beginning in the 1930's that worsened after the riots of 1968. The area was transformed by new urban development in the 1990's and is once again a center of the city's music and cultural scene.

A Poet Walks into a Bookstore on U Street, Circa 2008

she tells me they
only sell books about

social justice and
peace and that mine are mostly

about love and
relationships which they

don't promote.
i ask her if she thought

changing the world by
herself was such a good

idea and how could you ever
be free without

someone to hold
i wonder how many

revolutions started with a
kiss how many communists Neruda

made love to how free it must
feel to walk through life

at peace
alone

JANE ALBERDESTON CORALÍN (1968 –)

Jane Alberdeston Coralín was born in Puerto Rico and raised in Washington, DC, and has returned to the island of her birth to teach English at the University of Puerto Rico. She is co-author of the novel *Sister Chicas*, and is a Cave Canem fellow. HR-57 is a club on 14th St. NW, also known as the Center for the Preservation of Jazz and Blues. It takes its name from the 1987 House Resolution designating jazz music as a national American treasure.

For Black Girls Who Don't Know
Amiri Baraka at HR-57, Washington DC, 1995

I was a girl who knew nothing
Of jazz. Just another girl in line, waiting for you to read
The rest of a twenty volume suicide note.
What did I know of your coming music,
Your blue-banded heart, slit-gong tongue,
Hepcat in all your bones. I was a girl
Who knew nothing of love supreme, still stuck
In her papi's lounge-singer record scratches.
How you would leave me shook, body
A gourd in the hands of egun-eguns, dug up
For song, rolled under my skins,
Tripping me up, rocks in my soles,
Forgetting me how to heel-toe.
You walk in hot,
Hot with flu, 103 degrees of hot
And climbing mountains
In your strut, hands fast and flailing,
Flinging words with sweat, cool,
But not yet hot like cool.
You step up in that right knee strut,
Heathens!
Stage-stride in a broken line,
Your body stamping out a long-lost morse code.
Freedom Jazz, you call it and
Throw your shoulders back,
Back against the band's yielding riffs,
Bent back, as if your poem were a sax against your lips,
Reaching towards the ceiling for legroom.
What shaman in your staccato, hand smacking leg,

As if all of you were made of word,
Tapping the air, our ears, the wall with bop,
Backbeat, timbale, crisp lettuce sound.
You start the long Whoooooo towards eeee
And I think of the dizzy ways we mourn.
Blood confetti storms, scattering.
Right there in that moment, I loved you.
You with your eyes closed against the room,
As if you could make that horn just be.

REBECCA VILLARREAL (1969 -)

Rebecca Villarreal is a poet and visual artist, formerly of DC, now living in Chicago, whose work has been featured in *The Washington Post* and *The Chicago Tribune*. The Smithsonian Folklife Festival is a free, annual outdoor festival held on the National Mall (between 7th Street and 14th Street) for two weeks each summer, highlighting the food, arts, and folkways of different cultures in the US and abroad.

After the Rains

one moment on seventh street

you just passed the go-go plastic bucket man
surrounded by Wisconsin tourists
buckling bony knees to the beat
smell rain-soaked grass, bush, even fir tree

buses on seventh street
conduct a symphony
tempo and rhythm
sweep up children's laughter
punctuated by passing lunchtime conversation

oh the celebration of sun
preparation for Folklife Festival
with Mali brick houses
water them green hose

breathe in and out this moment
whistling with breakpads, songbirds
and the crush of sand and pebbles underfoot

VENUS THRASH (1969 –)

Venus Thrash is an adjunct teacher at Trinity Washington University, and has published in *Gargoyle, Folio, Torch,* the *Arkansas Review*, and *Beltway Poetry Quarterly*. The nickname "Chocolate City" originated with 1970's disc jockeys, to refer to the city's majority African-American population. Malcolm X Park, on 16th Street in the Columbia Heights neighborhood, was formerly known as Meridian Hill because it was located on the exact longitude of the city's original milestone marker, a geographic line thought to command considerable spiritual power (which explains why so many churches and two Masonic temples are located on 16th Street as well).

Thicker Than Water

for Tim

We are fierce
adventurers crisscrossing
Chocolate City,

hitting clubs just after sundown,
avoiding big-armed bouncers
demanding money at the door.

We traverse more terrain
in search of sin
than John Newton sailed

on the Middle passage
hauling human cargo.
We sing Amazing Grace

Before a black, gay God
on back row pews we bless
with our own holy water.

Our dark kisses
thick and humid
as DC summer nights.

We stand as the Sphinx
by the dawn of day,
built of ashes and dust,

Malcolm X Park, our Giza.
We are Pharaohs –
untouched, unharmed by time

or haters of men like us.
You, Khafre. I, Djedfre. Brothers.
In war. In blood. In love.

We have been here before,
our brown bodies laid bare,
embraced in the warmth

of this ancient sun.

PAULETTE BEETE (1970 -)

Paulette Beete is the author of a poetry chapbook, *Blues for a Pretty Girl*.
Her honors include an Intro Award for Fiction from the Association of Writers
and Writing Programs, and a winter writing fellowship from the Fine Arts
Work Center. She describes the residential neighborhood of Petworth,
where trains coming into Union Station from the east can sometimes be
heard in the distance.

Shepherd Street, NW. Back Porch. Night.

A porch. Night. A train howls in the distance. A rocking chair on that porch, a woman in
that chair, her voice between howl & moan caught.   That chair safe as

a train testifying there is always somewhere else.

The woman's howl, fierce & empty as the night she holds in her lap, braiding its long swift hair. The train's leaving anchors the soft edges of her lap, the raw

crease where chair meets hip. She's hungered several years, lighting candles

as if for a baby or a painless goodbye. She's braiding hooks & anchors to the swift hair of night, pulling past tenderness.   Her own hair smelled once like smoke

& aftershave, everywhere. There was a season of moaning, when she didn't hunger

trains. There is hunger here & something difficult to hold. There is the tug & pull of hands against glass, waving through windows at bodies indistinguishable from grass.

                              This is what trembles the lip between
first silence & next silence. *This is night*, someone tells her. *No, I don't hear any trains.*

REGIE CABICO (1970 -)

Regie Cabico is a National Poetry Slam champion, and co- editor of *Poetry Nation: The North American Anthology of Fusion Poetry*. He is artistic director of Sol y Soul, and the DC Youth Slam coach. The W Hotel, formerly the Hotel Washington, is located on 15th Street across from the US Treasury, and is famous for the view from its rooftop bar. Halo is a bar on P Street NW in the Logan Circle neighborhood. The "gay sauna" is the nearby Crew Club on 14th Street NW.

DC August Love Songs

From the W hotel bar,
we drink pale ale & stare

at the tiny watchmen
standing on the White House roof.

With your cell phone,
I photograph the monument
so it comes out of your ear.

        *

We stroll Chinatown's fake brick
& plastic letterings.

Romance does not need a gentrified
mall but a man who makes him laugh

by rubbing his nose up the Gallery Place
escalator, amidst the homophobic

preachers dressed like Ninja Turtles.

*

On the Foggy Bottom shuttle,
We exchange our greatest sex stories.

You, a three-way in Spain.
Me, outside a bodega.

You ask what my most loving
intimate sexual moment was,

I can't remember a whole-hearted
loving moment. When we step

onto the Kennedy Center
Roof Terrace, we step into

a mirage, our balls sweating
up a storm.

*

I read your poems at Halo bar.
It's lit like the inside of a Xerox machine.

You dislike your poems
& have the urge to visit the gay sauna.

Its fancy, you say, *& too bright!*
I sit wrapped in a towel watching 70's porn.

Ay papi, papi! from the closets.
I wonder if you had anything
to do with making those cries.

I feel like a bipolar mermaid.
You tell me you see a magical Puck.

*

Why did you cry when you took me to the airport?
I felt too small for your words.

I fucked a comedian in San Francisco.
Was his timing good?

My therapist told me not to break your heart.
What if you did?

The monuments can't be romantic
when there are mosquitoes

I would've cuddled if it wasn't so hot.

*

He leaves behind
a swig of Southern Comfort
& a half-eaten apple.

A swinging door attached to my
bedroom opens into a smaller bedroom.

The pillow cases we slept on
become tiny flags, waved by the window,
the approaching September
breeze in the merciless swamp heat.

Flags of surrender or celebration.
Our heads side by side.

The dozen roses I bundled in a tiny pitcher.

SAMUEL MIRANDA (1970 -)

Samuel Miranda hosts the Sabor Sundays reading series and has published poems in *Chiron Review, Beltway Poetry*, and the *DC Poets Against the War* anthology. He works for the DC Commission for the Arts. Bacon's Funeral Home is also located in Columbia Heights. The neighborhood is majority African-American and Latino, and has gentrified considerably since a new Metro station opened in 1999.

Bacon's Funeral Home, 13th Street

In Bacon's Funeral Home
the young are on display.
Painted up like showgirls
and dressed in Sunday best
they wait in a darkened room.
Their visitors arrive,
climbing the narrow staircase
they crowd into the tight space
where flowers cannot
mask the scent
of mourning
and *despedida*
is a silent prayer.

Outside others wait their turn.

Sitting on the low brick wall
they smoke Newports
and clasp hands with new arrivals.
Some pace, red eyed
mourning the dead
and their own lives
which they have spent
arm in arm
with young men
who in life are ghosts
and in death
become photos they carry
between thick fingers.

Hands gripping bottles
of Hennessy and Chivas
turn the open mouths
towards the ground,
they pour the first shot
onto the concrete,
losing themselves
in the burning
of the shots that follow.
"Ashes to ashes and dust to dust,"
whispers a young man.
His eyes watch the wind
swirling the brown leaves
and small bits of paper
that litter the ground.

HAYES DAVIS (1972 -)

Hayes Davis teaches high school English at Sidwell Friends School. His poetry
has appeared in such journals as *New England Review, Poet Lore, Gargoyle,*
and *Beltway Poetry Quarterly*. He describes a quiet winter drive through the
Shaw neighborhood.

Shine

The last night in February was warm.
A light rain clouded around street lamps,
creating rainbow mists that colored avenues
different shades of empty Sunday night.

The absence of activity outside the car
made The Roots' new CD reach
out of the speakers, distracting our ears
from the squeak of the pothole-weary

front axle with crisp taps on the side
of the snare, brisk walks on the high hat
laced under Black Thought's gentle verbal
jabs. As we drove slowly through the quiet

city, brothas started to appear on every corner.
The youngest in the first group rapped the last verse
of "Double Trouble" and his voice possessed
a peace that matched the night. I hadn't heard

such calm in a long while, or seen smiles
like those fixed on the faces of his friends,
so far from the frowns and scowls on the covers
of Vibe, Blaze, The Source. On the next corner,

black men young and old discussed
the fallacy of a released but vote-less felon,
the elusive ghost of owning an acre, let alone
forty, and the displacement inherent

in urban development. I won't tell you
how refreshing it was to hear what I heard—
But I slept more quietly that night, waking
only to look out at the street lights.

YVETTE NEISSER MORENO (1973 -)

Yvette Neisser Moreno translates poetry from Spanish, Hebrew, and Arabic, and her translations of the poems of Luis Alberto Ambroggio are published in *Difficult Beauty: Selected Poems*. She teaches poetry and translation at The Writer's Center and has taught poetry in public schools in Maryland, Virginia, and DC. The X2 bus runs from just west of the White House, across downtown on H Street, to Benning Road NE.

The Slow Passage to Anacostia

If I stare long enough into the relentless dark,
the X2 pulls to the corner, opens its tired jaw
and pushes ahead lurch by lurch
into the resistance of H Street: dusk

sinking into sidewalks and take-out delis,
hot dog vendors in empty lots,
liquor store cashiers sealed behind glass.
And within this moving husk, fifty strangers

confined together but for the door
that cringes open at each stop.
Headphones spill faint rhythms
into the bus's half-silence, the steady hum

of engine droning on pavement
where no one speaks above the clink
of coins in the machine—until one man's voice
pierces thick air, cursing

the slow passage to Anacostia,
cursing left turns and lights fading to yellow.
No one lifts an eye except
to gaze through scratched windows.

Outside, the usual: kids strutting,
shouting their own praises, streaming off
the football field or out of church,
one car radio blaring rap at a stoplight—

and here, one man's voice is a cry of longing
to which no one will listen—
a cry of stasis, of unlit bus stops
and forsaken destinations,

of the tense space between a man and woman
waiting on a winter day. And still,
the X2 follows H Street all the way
to the city's edge until something pulls

its wheels like a magnet
back into the gridded patterns of Northeast,
where this man's cry lingers like a vibration
caught between the hum and the ear.

KEN RUMBLE (1974 -)

Ken Rumble was born in DC, raised in Chevy Chase, MD, and now lives in Durham, NC. He is the author of the book *Key Bridge*, and a member of the 715 Washington Artist Collective. Lake Artemisia was named in the 1890's for Artemisia Drefs, wife of an early surveyor. When the Metro expanded into Prince George's County in 1972, the lake was expanded, and Drefs's granddaughter, also named Artemisia, donated the land to the Capital Park and Planning Commission.

from Key Bridge

8. april. 2001

Lake Artemisia
blue bubbles, map's bladders—
mouth of Anacostia River,
way up & out
        (*out out (damned spot*
In Maryland:
in the loop, the ring
I-495.
Off most D.C.
      (meaning federal
maps, that lake drains down
        (*Artemisia—genus of plants distinguished by a*
        (*peculiarly bitter or aromatic taste, including the*
        (*common wormwood, mugwort & southernwood*
        (*Artemis—Diana, huntress goddess of the moon*
          (what do these things concern
            (with a depression in the land
              (water pools into,
                a location (ripples
follows a ragged wave of green down
the map past Brentwood, Colman Manor, Sheverly & on
into the District, widening under Benning,
Sousa, Douglass & 11th Street Bridge, carves D.C.
to a pair of barbs where it mingles
with the Potomac loses its name mixes
off the map into the room silt & minnows slosh
across the hardwood floors dirty pants swirl
in the slight current the bed goes dark & wet

cools knees laps ribs swells
books like bellies sweeps the page ink into faint
black clouds wets beard eyes ears breath
buoyant enough to float
a few feet off the floor

KATY RICHEY (1974 -)

Katy Richey is a high school English teacher and co-host of the monthly
Sunday Kind of Love Readings Series at Busboys and Poets. She has
published poems in *Rattle, Gargoyle, Torch,* and *Beltway Poetry Quarterly.*
The Smithsonian National Museum of Natural History, built in 1911, is
famous for its Hall of Mammals and its Insect Zoo, among other exhibits.

Natural history

The Savana smells like wax
newly buffed to shine.
Impala teetering
          on stilettos,
leap from plexiglass.

Centipedes
with curved mustaches
rove on vacant shells
of kinkajou bones,
sitting like noble tombstones.

Loud children
with plastic-museum-charms
slap the glass at water buffalo
          holding black comma
nostrils high.

They're not moved.
The children are only
a whisper of wind awry.
If this is an intrusion,
nature is unaware.

Teri Ellen Cross (1974 -)

Teri Ellen Cross has been featured in numerous anthologies, including *Bum Rush the Page, Gathering Ground, Growing Up Girl,* and *Poetic Voices Without Borders 2.* She is Poetry and Lectures Coordinator at the Folger Shakespeare Library. The Beltway Sniper attacks by John Allen Williams and Lee Boyd Malvo took place over three weeks in October 2002. The randomness of the attacks scared many in the region, and many schools cancelled field trips and outdoor activities. The youngest victim, Iran Brown, described here, was shot in front of his Middle School in Bowie, MD. He survived.

Call me God

In 2002, a sniper terrorized the Washington DC metro region, killing ten, wounding six. The sniper's eighth victim was a 13-year-old boy, shot in the abdomen on October 7 in Prince George's County, MD. His aunt, a nurse, rushed him to a nearby hospital. At the crime scene authorities discovered a shell casing as well as a Tarot card (the Death card) inscribed with the phrase, "Call me God" on the front.

Calm, the steady brook of words
don't worry baby, it's gon' be okay, itsgonbeokay.
    She had always been the baby.
Her older sister cooler, longer legs, bigger friends,
but their teddy bears, their Barbies, shared the same adventures,
same Barbie mansion, shared mommies.
Now her peripheral cradles her nephew.
He moans in the passenger seat, the bullet, his blood,
crimson shouts on the white of his football uniform.
She rocks herself, driving, rocking.
The lane clears to the left, and she is there-
watching him slide from the fluid between her sister's legs
watching him climb over the couch, surf the car seat, bold, unbroken.
His breathing is shallow, ragged, shock rides up on him,
here, her training takes over
keep pressure on it baby, pressure, constant pressure.
Her foot caresses the gas pedal, coaxes more speed.
When your sister hands you her baby—you promise,
you hold him close, you coo, you let him sleep with you—six month-old feet
kick you in the back, you see the family nose in that tiny face,

you see your dimples in his cheeks, you watch that round, fuzzy head bobble,
weave, duck, your hand the constant safety-net behind it.
When you sister hands you her baby, says *can you drop him off at school,
it's on the way to your job*, you say *sure*, you say *fine*, you think
of the work day, the asshole doctors, your packed tuna sandwich,
you think you will hand him back to her, whole.

FRED JOINER (1975 -)

Fred Joiner is the host of the HOME reading series at Hillyer Art Space, and
the curator of Intersections, the reading series hosted by the American Poetry
Museum. He lives in the historic Anacostia neighborhood, which he describes
here. Two Metro buses bisect the neighborhood: the 94 from east to west, and
the 90 from north to south.

Song for Anacostia

The 94 hums
up the rough side
of Stanton.

Washington View's
open windows blare
drums in the pocket,
the breakdown
of the perfect groove.

The 90 salsas across town
into the forgotten
bottom of DC,

a car alarm echoes its
protest on MLK

two porch griots wail
their pain and pity.

On the corner,
two preachers
can be heard
through the sanctuary walls,

one reading scripture,
the other raptured in a moan.

The smell of last night's first drink
poured out in a crooning ballad
for the missed and missing
        a song for a father,

a song for a mother unchilded,

a song for a child
playing ahead of the beat,
a nursery rhyme
for every teddy bear
rooted at a street sign.

This is the sound of blues breaking
the broken, back together;
the sound of chaos, organizing;
the sound of breath forming
words in vinyl's backspin

these are the sounds
gathered in blood,
shed for remission of
silence and sadness.

DEIDRE R. GANTT (1976 –)

Dierdre Gantt (also known as Hadassah Ayodele), teaches at Prince George's Community College, where she is faculty advisor for the student literary magazine. She writes a monthly column for *East of the River* newspaper, and is a member of the Ward 7 Arts Collaborative. Clay Street NE is located in the Lincoln Heights neighborhood near where Benning Road and East Capitol Street intersect.

Clay Street Cantata

    squeeze the metronome

              it did not take a symphony

of shell casings to puncture
the silence of my evening nap

cue screech of tire
cue unintelligible wail
andante
andante

just seven shots
an overture of evil intentions
tapped so close to my window
I think I taste gunpowder
but it's really blood spurting
from my tongue   pierced
by a bandolier of canines and incisors

cue paddy wagon
cue beating copter blades
allegro
allegro

(with feeling)
we don't know nothing, man
we just headin to the carryout
we ain't see who crashed homegirl's whip
we ain't see who fired up that truck
why you worried about what's in my pockets
we ain't do nothin to nobody

moments later
back flattened against the sofa base
elbow slack upon the cool, pine floor
metaphors ooze, trickle
find each other   and form
inky puddles on a nearby page:

you heard about shorty up the block
feds ran up in his baby momma spot
found his weed sacks
crack water
pistols like war comin
his kids gon' be grown
by the time he get home

cue sofa dragged onto sidewalk
cue wild-blooming offspring

> an ode to the ears
> whose sanity and survival depend
> on deafness to the daily assaults
> of well-armed orchestras

squeeze the metronome

> an elegy for the fingers
> who massage these instruments
> and call their awful rhythm
> music

grave
grave

DERRICK WESTON BROWN (1976 -)

Derrick Weston Brown is the Langston Hughes Poet-in-Residence at Busboys and Poets, and teaches children in Southeast DC. The Metro system, administered by the Washington Metropolitan Area Transit Authority, operates five color-coded lines with 86 stations and over 106 miles of track.

Missed Train

> I smelled you at the Metro stop
> Tasted you on the Yellow
> Glimpsed you on the Green
> Caught you on the Orange
> Loved you on the Red
> Lost you on the Blue,
>
> Now I need a transfer
> or at least exit fare,
> cause no one deserves
> to take such a ride,
> and end up being taken
> for every dime.

Baby you a last minute change of plans,
an unexpected phone call at the God hour
that leaves me feeling mortal.

HOLLY BASS (1976 -)

Holly Bass is a freelance journalist, and a performance artist known for her
dynamic solo shows that combine poetry, music, and movement. She is the
Countee Cullen Poet-in-Residence at Busboys and Poets. Before the gentrifi-
cation of Logan Circle in the early 2000's, it was known as a place to find
drugs and prostitutes.

the stroll

remember Logan Circle
before the Whole Foods and
Studio Theatre took up
residence with their
neon and gleam

when it was impossible
to hail a cab and after the party
at your friend's group house
you gave up and walked home

friday night, 3am, up 15th
cars snaking across Mass Ave
the girls in bikini tops
hot pink hot pants
and perhaps, if it was cold,
tight tiny fake fur jackets
over swimwear and lingerie

the parade of Lucite heels
lavender-shadowed eyes
cherry smash lips
torsos leaning into car windows
selling simultaneously
from the front and the back

the stroll in its glory days

to me it seemed a carnival
an endless celebration
this parade of Peaches and Destinys
and Cocos and Desirees...

NATALIE E. ILLUM (1976 -)

Natalie Illum is a founding member of Mothertongue, a DC women's spoken word venue, and coordinator of 3Word Productions, which promotes queer and marginalized artists. She has performed widely at festivals and slam competitions across the US. The DC statehood movement, begun in 1971, advocates making the District of Columbia a US state, so citizens would get full representation in the US Congress and full control over local affairs.

Yoga

My neighbor's life was spared
by an air conditioner; the bullet
wouldn't go through. But we

were malleable. Love, you
turned the wailing wall
of my heart into
a white flag. Gave me
blossoms that fell
too soon – a metaphor
for our future. I'm still afraid
of an alchemy that bleeds.
I am not

Palestine. Lover, you showed me
that I am not worth your accord.
But I believed in

your outstretched hand;
the gravel of love
on your barren tongue.

You held me in the rubble of
our district; promised me
a miracle of statehood
then exhaled any intention.

When we were
finally obliterated,
your eyes almost
reflected peace.

MAUREEN THORSON (1978 -)

Maureen Thorson is a lawyer, and the author of three chapbooks, including
Twenty Questions for the Drunken Sailor and *Mayport*. She is the publisher
and editor of Big Game Books, and co-curator of the In Your Ear Reading
Series. Jay Rockefeller (D-WV) is the great-grandson of the oil tycoon John
D. Rockefeller, America's first billionaire.

K Street Interview

Did you know? Did you know?
                     Did you know?—
John D. Rockefeller IV, America's favored son,
        descendant
    of a bigamist snake oil salesman
       and you know what that makes him—

              a slick son of a bitch who doesn't mind who he fucks over!

Oh, John D., you're a senator, and
        so near
   to oil, so near to coal, and oh—

the men who interview me defend guys like you,
        they wear dark dull suits, these K Street types, the kind
that would make Randall Jarrell do a doubletake
    to see
    that nothing had changed since he wandered around
at the zoo, complaining to the buffalo.

These men, they've got shoulders like the hills
    of your constituent state, and we know:
        There's gold! Black gold! In them thar hills!
    and today

I've come for my share. That combustible honey.
It'll come, dark and sweet, right out of my mouth.
I'm going to cover these guys
    in petroleum. So move over, John D.

The octopus is back.

KYLE DARGAN (1980 -)

Kyle Dargan is the author of two books of poems, *The Listening* and *Bouquet of Hungers*, and teaches creative writing and literature at American University. The Greyhound Bus Station is located on First Street NE, just north of Union Station.

Boarding Points
Bus Station, NE DC

[N]

A baby is one less
bag you may carry.

[E]

The hustler's faded velour,
a tepid, alien hide—let him
take you home.

[S]

The NY direct, ever punctual
as it is never arriving
from anywhere. It grows
out the tarmac, wet to steaming.

[W]

"Hey poet, you got any papers?"
Shouldn't papers be laced with poems?

[S]

Some idle stiller than the coaches.

[E]

"I can't. At the department store
today, I bought a face. I owe them
this spare change."

[W]

When the busses stop,
these men will clean up
into princes, igniting night like
Montecristos kissed by razors.

[N]

The brother with the shakes
is suspicious of the bench.
He may be on to something.

[S]

The longest line: WILLIAMSBURG,
HAMPTON, NORFOLK, VIRGINIA BEACH.
Somewhere, coasts remember
the first vessel.

[E]

Industry: now
the beggar has a soda
and a straw.

[W]

The new shift at the ticket booth
wears a cotton phallus from her neck.
Over the p.a., she tames crowds.

[S]

Thunk—an infant Newton
jostles receivers from pay
phones' palms onto his skull.
Even against babies
there are laws.

REGINALD DWAYNE BETTS (1980 -)

Reginald Dwayne Betts is the author of the memoir *A Question of Freedom,*
and the forthcoming poetry collection *Shahid Reads His Own Palm.* He
teaches in the DC Creative Writing Workshop at Hart Middle School.
Mississippi Avenue SE runs from Washington Highlands to Hillcrest
Heights in Anacostia.

Elegy With A RIP Shirt Turning Into The Wind

Some days, the air turns away from me,
and I pray pistols into my hands, as if there
is a peace that will open up with bullets,
with the sound of gunshots. In the street,

the boys play a game they call throw
back. It is football, every man for himself as
he weaves under the wires above Mississippi
Avenue, his body juking like scythes below

the sneakers swinging. Call them fresh: Jordans,
Air Force 1s and Chuck Taylors singing
death songs when the wind blows hard enough.
Touchdowns are as rare as angels and when

the boy turns his body around so the RIP
shirt slants against the wind, there is
a moment when he is not weighed down
by gravity, when he owns the moment

as he crashes into the boys and they
all look like a dozen marionettes,
all controlled by the spinning sneaker
strings of the dead boys above them.

ALAN KING (1981 -)

Alan King is a regular at area open mics, and his poems have been published
in *Alehouse, Beltway Poetry Quarterly, Boxcar Review,* and *MiPoesias.* State
of the Union is a nightclub on U Street NW. U Street, famous for its jazz-era
clubs, went into an economic decline in the 1940's, suffered through four days
of urban rioting after the death of Martin Luther King, Jr. in 1968, then made
a comeback in the 1990's. It is now once again one of the premier areas in the
city to hear live music.

Invocation

Whatever happened...?
Times done changed.
     – De La Soul, "Super Emcees"

Ten bucks gets us beyond
the barricade of bouncers
into State of the Union for

Old Skool Hip Hop Fridays.
And something propels itself
around dark bodies swaying

to the bass-heavy current
of a DJ spinning golden era
from his vinyl looms.

That night, bodies crowded
the club like records stacked
inside a milk crate

under dim lights and a ceiling
sinking like the soggy bottom
of a cardboard box

straining from the weight of what
it carried. And what carries us
when all we have is the ghost

of a memory? – De La's
"Super Emcees" booming through
the totem of speakers.

ADAM PELLEGRINI (1984 -)

Adam Pellegrini is an MFA candidate in Poetry at the University of Maryland and co-editor of the journal *Cartographer Electric*. Lincoln Park, off East Capitol Street on Capitol Hill, is home to the first statue in Washington to honor President Abraham Lincoln: the Emancipation Memorial, designed by Thomas Ball in 1876. The statue depicts two figures, a standing Lincoln (with the Emancipation Proclamation in his right hand) and an African American male shackled and crouching at his feet. The poem describes the election night in 2008 when Barack Obama became the 44th US President.

In Lincoln Park, Election Night

Tonight, we've won, all of us. One man's voice
streams from TVs, holding apartments and rowhouses still—

rooms of ties & dresses & cold salads—holds them
like a drunk holds the warm ass of her last beer.

Tonight has brought Honest Abe back to us,
as if the dead could somehow still sing.

His voice—through doors & windows & out
& punched by ecstatic yelps & car horns

in the street—floats up. It bursts with firecrackers
now working their bright fingers in a tense sky,

& against these dark trees, neat gardens, brick sidewalks,
&, in a park up the street, in old Abe's own iron cheeks.

There, as forever, he hovers his hand above a kneeled,
half-naked iron boy—*emancipation, release,*

both figures lapped by light; as all around, beyond these blocks,
the City shoots its wad at a cool sliver-moon

& waits.

ABDUL ALI (1984 -)

Abdul Ali has published poems, reviews, and essays in *Essence, Black Issues Book Review, Gargoyle,* and *Beltway Poetry Quarterly*. He hosts the monthly radio show, "Poet's Corner" on WPFW-FM. DC historically has had a large population of Southern transplants, drawn to the city by job opportunities and the promise of affordable housing.

There Were Homes

hidden on every block
at least one I knew of

storied behind fire
hydrants that bled
mellifluous tap water
quenching
our colored thirst
on brick august sundays

cherry blossom induced naps
under plum colored heavens

the stairs with her chipped teeth
always welcoming our southern
footprints

the wet washington air
pregnant with
Negro uplift

II.
inside these homes
where a brick wall could
match Papa's forehead
(worry lines, mostly)
when he'd riff on the
stairs blowing donut holes
with his cuban cigar

we'd talk about Granddaddy Cornelius
who'd hum Precious Lord
as he waited for the milkman

& Great Granddaddy Ernest
who'd leave notes written on
easter sunday handkerchiefs

I am not a boy
I am not a boy

before going to work
at union station

how the Men
in my family found home
in a constellation of
northern stars

before u street got a facelift
jazz became an elevator tune
& apartments cost more than
our grandparents' brownstones

There
Were
Homes

Acknowledgments

Karren L. Alenier, "Against the Wall"
Reprinted from *Beltway Poetry Quarterly*, Vol. 9:4, 2008.

Elizabeth Alexander, "Early Cinema"
Reprinted from *Antebellum Dream Book*, Graywolf Press, 2001, with permission of Graywolf Press, Minneapolis, Minnesota.

Kwame Alexander, "A Poet Walks Into a Bookstore on U Street, Circa 2008"
Reprinted from *And Then You Know: New and Selected Poems*, Word of Mouth Books, 2009.

Abdul Ali, "There Were Homes"
Reprinted from *Beltway Poetry Quarterly*, Vol. 8:4, 2007.

Francisco Aragón, "To the President"
Reprinted from *Beltway Poetry Quarterly*, Vol. 8:3, 2007.

Naomi Ayala, "Restaurante Santa Rosa"
Reprinted from *Beltway Poetry Quarterly*, Vol. 7:3, 2006.

Jonetta Rose Barras, "There's Been a Killing in the Neighborhood"
Reprinted from *The Corner Is No Place for Hiding*, Forest Woods Media Productions, 1996.

Derrick Weston Brown, "Missed Train"
Reprinted from *Beltway Poetry Quarterly*, Vol. 7:6, 2006.

Sterling A. Brown, "Glory, Glory"
Reprinted from the *Collected Poems of Sterling A. Brown,* TriQuarterly Books/ Northwestern University Press, 1989, with permission from John L. Dennis on behalf of the author's family.

Sarah Browning, "The Fifth Fact"
Reprinted from *Whiskey in the Garden of Eden*, The Word Works, 2007.

Kenneth Carroll, "Snookie Johnson Goes Down to the Recruiter's Office Near Benning Road and Starts Some Shit"
Reprinted from *Beltway Poetry Quarterly*, Vol. 1:2, 2000.

Grace Cavalieri, "Mapping DC"
Reprinted from *Beltway Poetry Quarterly,* Vol. 8:4, 2007.

William Claire, "The Jello Man on the Feast of the Circumcision"
Reprinted from *William Claire Poems: A Selection*, Turning Point Press, 2004.

Jane Alberdeston Coralin, "For Black Girls Who Don't Know"
Reprinted from *Proud Flesh: New Afrikan Journal of Culture, Politics and Consciousness,* Issue 6, 2007.

Ed Cox, "Evening News"
Reprinted from *Collected Poems*, Paycock Press, 2001, with permission from Laura Lunsford on behalf of the author's family.

Ramola D, "I Saw Her Rise"
Reprinted from *Beltway Poetry Quarterly*, Vol. 8:4, 2007.

Kyle Dargan, "Boarding Points"
Reprinted from *Bouquet of Hungers*, University of Georgia Press, 2007.

Ann Darr, "Temple on the Beltway Opens to the Media"
Reprinted from *Cleared for Landing*, Dryad Press, 1978, with permission from Deborah Darr on behalf of the author's family.

Tina Darragh, "Cliché as place—rainbows"
Originally published as Part III of *Pi in the Skye*, Ferguson & Franzino, 1980. Reprinted from *Striking Resemblance: Work 1980-1986*, Burning Deck, 1989.

Thulani Davis, "Rogue & Jar: 4/17/77"
Reprinted from *All The Renegade Ghosts Rise*, Anemone Press, 1978.

Tim Dlugos, "Swede"
Reprinted from *Powerless: Selected Poems 1973-1990*, edited by David Trinidad, High Risk Books, 1996. Copyright 1996 by the Estate of Tim Dlugos; reprinted by permission of the Estate of Tim Dlugos.

Thomas Sayers Ellis, "Tambourine Tommy"
Reprinted from *The Maverick Room*, Graywolf Press, 2005.

Roland Flint, "Poem Beginning & Ending O"
Reprinted from *And Morning*, Dryad Press, 1975, with permission from Dryad Press and Rosalind Cowie, on behalf of the author's family.

Sunil Freeman, "The Cinematographer's Dream"
Reprinted from *Surreal Freedom Blues*, Argonne Hotel Press, 1999.

David Gewanter, "War Bird: A Journal"
Reprinted from *War Bird,* University of Chicago Press, 2009.

Brian Gilmore, "Billy Eckstine Comes to Washington, D.C."
Reprinted from *Beltway Poetry Quarterly*, Vol. 7:3, 2006.

Barbara Goldberg, "Once, the Buffalo"
Reprinted from *The Royal Baker's Daughter*, University of Wisconsin Press, 2008.

Patricia Gray, "Washington Days"
Reprinted from *Innisfree Poetry Journal*, Vol. 1, 2005.

Michael Gushue, "Big Ben's Liquors"
Reprinted from *Beltway Poetry Quarterly*, Vol. 7:3, 2006.

O.B. Hardison, Jr., "Pro Musica Antiqua"
Reprinted from *Pro Musica Antiqua*. Baton Rouge: Louisiana State University Press, 1977, with permission from Marifrancis Hardison, on behalf of the author's family.

Essex Hemphill, "Family Jewels"
Reprinted from *Tongues Untied*, edited by Martin Humphries, Gay Men's Publishers Ltd./Alyson Publications, 1987, with permission from the Frances Goldin Agency.

Randall Horton, "Marvin Gaye Sings the National Anthem at the NBA All-Star Game"
Reprinted from *The Lingua Franca of Ninth Street*, Main Street Rag, 2009.

Esther Iverem, "Second Inauguration"
Reprinted from *Living in Babylon*, Africa World Press, 2006.

Gray Jacobik, "Forgetting David Weinstock"
Reprinted from *The Double Task*, University of Massachusetts Press, 1998.

Brandon D. Johnson, "Displaced Person"
Reprinted from *The Strangers Between*, Tell Me Somethin Books, 1999.

Percy E. Johnston, Jr., "Blaupunkt"
Reprinted from *Dasein*, 1976; used by permission of Howard University, Moorland-Spingarn Archives.

Fred Joiner, "Song for Anacostia"
Reprinted from *Beltway Poetry Quarterly*, Vol. 7:3, 2006.

Beth Joselow, "Stands"
Reprinted from *Begin at Once*, Chax Press, 2007.

Michael Lally, "from DC"
Reprinted from *Hollywood Magic*, Little Caesar Press, 1982.

Mary Ann Larkin, "Labor Day at the Shrine of Our Lady"
Reprinted from *Beltway Poetry Quarterly*, Vol. 7:3, 2006.

Toni Asante Lightfoot, "Mothership Future Dream Palabramorphetic"
Reprinted from *Ariel II of Triton College*, Spring 2009.

Saundra Rose Maley, "War Bonds"
Reprinted from *Dryad*, Vol. 12, 1975.

David McAleavey, "She had a vision"
Reprinted from *Huge Haiku*, Chax Press, 2005.

Richard McCann, "Banners"
Reprinted from *Ghost Letters*, Alice James Books, 1994.

Eugene J. McCarthy, "Dulles Airport"
Reprinted from *Selected Poems*, Lone Oak Press, 1997 with permission from
Lone Oak Press, an Imprint of Finney Company, Lakeville, MN.

Judith McCombs, "Consider Poplar Point"
Reprinted from *Beltway Poetry Quarterly*, Vol. 9.2, 2008.

E. Ethelbert Miller, "Elizabeth Keckley: 30 Years a Slave and 4 Years in the
White House"
Reprinted from *First Light: New and Selected Poems*, Black Classic Press, 1994.

May Miller, "The Washingtonian"
Reprinted from *Dust of Uncertain Journey*, Lotus Press, 1975, with permission
from Dr. Miller Newman on behalf of the author's family.

Miles David Moore, "Full Moon on K Street"
Reprinted from *The Bears of Paris*, The Word Works, Inc., 1995.

Yvette Neisser Moreno, "The Slow Passage to Anacostia"
Reprinted from *Beltway Poetry Quarterly*, Vol. 7:3, 2006.

Kathi Morrison-Taylor, "Bomb Pop"
Reprinted from *Beltway Poetry Quarterly*, Vol. 7:3, 2006.

Jose Emilio Pacheco, "Two Poems on Sligo Creek"
Poem in Spanish first appeared in *Cuidad de la memoria*, Ediciones Era,
1989. English translation by Cynthia Steele reprinted from *City of Memory and
Other Poems*, City Lights, 1997.

Betty Parry, "Daisy's Garden"
Reprinted from *Shake the Parrot Cage*, New Poets Series, Inc., 1994, with
permission from Brian Parry on behalf of the author's family.

Linda Pastan, "At the Udvar-Hazy Airplane Museum, Chantilly, Virginia"
Reprinted from *Queen of a Rainy Country*, W.W. Norton & Co., 2006. Copyright
2006 by Linda Pastan, used by permission of W.W. Norton & Company, Inc.

Richard Peabody, "I'm in Love with the Morton Salt Girl"
Reprinted from *I'm in Love with the Morton Salt Girl*, Paycock Press, 1979; re-
vised edition, Paycock Press, 1985.

Elizabeth Poliner, "Students Painting in the Community Garden on Newark Street"
Reprinted from *Folio*, Volume 21, Issue 2, Spring 2006.

Minnie Bruce Pratt, "Sharp Glass"
Reprinted from *The Dirt She Ate: New and Selected Poems*, University of
Pittsburgh Press, 2003.

Liam Rector, "Twenty-four"
Reprinted from *The Executive Director of the Fallen World*, Univ. of Chicago
Press, 2006, with permission from Tree Swenson on behalf of the author's family.

Joan Retallack, "Present Tensed"
Reprinted from *Memnoir,* The Post-Apollo Press, 2004.

Joseph Ross, "The Universal Artificial Limb Company"
Reprinted from *Beltway Poetry Quarterly*, Vol. 8:4, 2007.

Ken Rumble, "8. april. 2001"
Reprinted from *Key Bridge*, Carolina Wren Press, 2007.

Robert Sargent, "Two Ways"
Reprinted from *The Cartographer,* Forest Woods Media Productions, 1994, with
permission from Mary Jane Barnett on behalf of the author's family.

Gregg Shapiro, "The Fortune Cookie"
Reprinted from *Protection, Gival Press*, 2008.

Alan Spears, "It's Amazing What You Get Used To"
Reprinted from *Gargoyle*, Issue 48, 2004.

Sharan Strange, "Saint on the Southbound S2: Ode to a Bus Driver"
Reprinted from *Callaloo,* Vol. 26, No. 2, 2003.

A.B. Spellman, "On Hearing Gonzalo Rubalcaba at Blues Alley"
Reprinted from *Things I Must Have Known*, Coffee House Press, 2008.

Hilary Tham, "Mrs. Wei on Governments"
Reprinted from *Bad Names for Women*, The Word Works, Inc., 1989, with permission from Joe Goldberg on behalf of the author's family.

Venus Thrash, "Thicker Than Water"
Reprinted from *Beltway Poetry Quarterly*, Vol. 8:3, 2007.

Dan Vera, "Ode to the Black Nationalist Pharoah Head of Georgia Avenue"
Reprinted from *The Space Between Our Danger and Delight*, Beothuk Books, 2009.

Belle Waring, "Storm Crossing Key Bridge"
Reprinted from Refuge, *University of Pittsburgh Press*, 1990. Reprinted by permission of the University of Pittsburgh Press.

Joshua Weiner, "National Pastime"
Reprinted from *The Book of Giants*, University of Chicago Press, 2006.

Reed Whittemore, "The Destruction of Washington"
Reprinted from *The Feel of Rock: Poems of Three Decades,* Dryad Press, 1982.

Ahmos Zu-Bolton II, "Taxicab Blues"
Reprinted from *Synergy: An Anthology of Washington, D.C. Blackpoetry*, edited by Ahmos Zu-Bolton II and E. Ethelbert Miller, Energy BlackSouth Press, 1975.

Beltway Poetry Quarterly is an online journal and resource bank founded in January 2000 by Kim Roberts. We strive to showcase the richness and diversity of Washington area authors in every issue, with poets from different backgrounds, races, ethnicities, ages, and sexual orientations represented. We have included Pulitzer Prize winners and those who have never previously published. We publish academic, spoken word, and experimental authors—and also those poets whose work defies categorization. *Beltway Poetry* is also committed to documenting the region's rich literary history, as well as providing monthly updates to serve the needs of the literary community in the greater DC region. Subscriptions are free.

www.beltwaypoetry.com

Plan B Press is an independent publisher of emerging poets. Specializing in chapbooks, Plan B Press produces high-quality, distinctive books by some of the best under-published poets. It continues to grow and define itself by not only the authors that it publishes, but also by its readers. Many Plan B Press books incorporate highly visual components, while also encouraging further collaborations with artists from other mediums in exhibitions and performances that go beyond traditional poetic form. Founded in 1998, Plan B Press is headed by stevenallenmay.

www.planbpress.com

ABOUT THE EDITOR

KIM ROBERTS is the editor of the online journal *Beltway Poetry Quarterly* and author of two books of poems, *The Kimnama* (Vrzhu Press, 2007), and *The Wishbone Galaxy* (Washington Writers Publishing House, 1994). She has published widely in literary journals throughout the US, as well as in Canada, Ireland, France, Brazil, India, and New Zealand.

Poems by Roberts have been set to music by an alternative rock band, Arc of Ones, and by classical composer Daron Hagen, and several have been choreographed by Jane Franklin Dance Company. Individual poems of hers have been translated into Spanish, Portuguese, German, and Mandarin.

Roberts has done extensive research on writers with ties to Washington, DC. She has developed walking tours of Walt Whitman's Washington (co-written with Martin G. Murray, Rainbow History, 2005), Zora Neale Hurston's Washington (Humanities Council of Washington, 2007), and The Harlem Renaissance in DC (Split This Rock Festival, 2008). She was the Coordinator of a city-wide festival in 2005, "DC Celebrates Whitman: 150 Years of *Leaves of Grass*" sponsored by the Washington Friends of Walt Whitman.

Roberts is the recipient of grants from the National Endowment for the Humanities, the DC Commission on the Arts, and the Humanities Council of Washington. She has been awarded writers' residencies from twelve artist colonies. In 2008, she was given the Independent Voice Award from the Capitol Book Fest.

www.kimroberts.org

First Edition
Published 2010 by Plan B Press
Printed in the United States of America

Plan B Press
www.planbpress.com

Cover design by Katy Jean May
Book set in Times New Roman and Capitals